Ho
Not to
Say Mass

A Guidebook on Liturgical Principles and the Roman Missal

Revised Edition

Dennis C. Smolarski, s.j.

Paulist Press
New York • Mahwah, N.J.

IMPRIMI POTEST
September 9, 2002
Very Rev. Thomas Smolich, S.J., Provincial
California Province, Society of Jesus

Cover design by Valerie Petro

Library of Congress Cataloging-in-Publication Data

Smolarski, Dennis Chester, 1947–
    1. How not to say Mass : a guidebook on liturgical principles and the Roman missal / Dennis C. Smolarski.—Rev. ed.
      p. cm.
    Includes bibliographical references.
    ISBN 0-8091-4164-7 (alk. paper)
    1. Mass—Celebration. 2. Catholic Church—Liturgy. I. Title.
BX2230.5.S67 2003
264'.02036—dc 22

2003017632

Published by Paulist Press
997 Macarthur Boulevard
Mahwah, New Jersey 07430

www.paulistpress.com

Printed and bound in the United States of America

CONTENTS

To my Jesuit brothers

who have vividly shown me

by their examples

both how to say Mass

and how not to say Mass!

PRENOTES

1. For easy reference, I have included, wherever possible, references to *Documents of the Liturgy: 1963–1979* published by The Liturgical Press. These are indicated by the letters DOL followed by the paragraph number found in that book. This method of cross-referencing is also used by the excellent Canadian publication, the *National Bulletin on Liturgy*.

Because the revised *General Instruction of the Roman Missal* (GIRM) contained in the 2002 third edition of the Roman Missal has renumbered the paragraphs of earlier versions of the GIRM and includes some significant changes from the version found in DOL, no such cross-references to the GIRM have been included.

2. This book is *not* exclusively geared for priests. It is directed to *all* who have an active role in the liturgy of the church, i.e., bishops, priests, deacons, lectors, acolytes, musicians, liturgy committee members, active Christians. A stance had to be taken, however, and I decided to address my remarks primarily toward priests who preside at the Eucharist. Nevertheless, these remarks, in many cases, can also be taken to heart by many others, for example, members of liturgy committees, those who preside at communion services where there is no resident priest. In many situations, a liturgy committee or liturgical coordinator may actually shape a given eucharistic liturgy, and the priest who presides merely follows a predetermined script, blindly (and sometimes inaccurately) believing that "they must know what they are doing."

My major concern is to awaken people, particularly priests who preside at the Eucharist, to the authentic celebration of the renewed Eucharist in the Roman Rite. I have not attempted, as some have done elsewhere, to suggest ways to *adapt* the Roman Rite to a "better" form. Because of this particular concern, readers associated with "progressive" communities may find the remarks that follow obvious or even boring, and wonder why so much effort went into a project with so little applicability. My experience, however, of liturgy since the post-Vatican II reforms has been different. A significant number of priests and Christians still seem to be woefully ignorant of the basics of liturgy, as judged from the externals of the (by-the-book) liturgies that are celebrated, and so, the remarks that follow are directed primarily to help them. Moreover, my experience has also been that *adapted* liturgies can be as unliturgical as "by-the-book" liturgies, when presided over by individuals (and assisted by other ministers) who do not have a true sense of the symbolic nature of the renewed liturgy and an appropriate sense of drama as applied to liturgical ministry and movement. Rewriting prayers, rearranging sections of the liturgy, reassigning liturgical roles will not, *of themselves,* lead to a "better" liturgy, if the foundations of liturgy are ignored, that is, if the leaders of the liturgy ignore the basic symbols and fundamental gestures involved in the 2000-year tradition of Christian worship. My hope is that this book will awaken the reader to those fundamental concerns, no matter what his or her background is like.

3. This revised edition is primarily an updating of the text of the 1986 edition of this book necessitated, in part, by the publication of the third edition of the Roman Missal in 2002 with the revised *General Instruction of the Roman Missal.* Thus, among other changes, all cross-references to the GIRM in the text are now to the 2002 version with its revised numbering (unless specifically noted otherwise). For convenience, in Appendix II there is a cross-reference listing giving references

to the previous versions of the GIRM with additional references to the older text as found in DOL.

The major changes in the 2002 GIRM (compared to the 1975 GIRM) consist of a renumbering of the paragraphs and an updating and clarifying of the text. Substantial changes are relatively few and do not affect the basic principles on which this book is based. In fact, as will be noted throughout the text and briefly in section 10, some of the changes in the 2002 GIRM give greater emphasis to fundamental liturgical principles.

In addition, since 1986, there have been several other books or documents promulgated by the Holy See or the U.S. Conference of Catholic Bishops, including the revised translation of the *Order of Christian Funerals,* the *Book of Blessings,* the *Catechism of the Catholic Church,* and *Built of Living Stones* (U.S. Bishops). Furthermore, certain terms (such as *ambo* or *Book of the Gospels*) have become part of the standard liturgical terminology, and the text has been updated to reflect the current usage. In a few cases, other minor additions and changes have been introduced. The majority of the text, however, remains unchanged from the 1986 edition.

INTRODUCTION

In the "good old days" (although many would debate how *good* they actually were), we (thought we) knew what the Mass was about—it was the mystery of transubstantiation—it was the sacrament of Communion. It "worked" *ex opere operato,* and since it was in Latin anyway, no one really had to worry about intelligibility or "style." *Symbol* was suspect—Protestants talked about Christ's "symbolic" presence in the eucharistic elements. But Catholics were concerned about "real" presence. Even though the *Baltimore Catechism* told us that "a sacrament is an outward sign, instituted by Christ, to give grace," not very many Catholics really took the meaning of "outward sign" too seriously. Sacraments were signs only insofar as they could be perceived by the senses. What was *really* important was the "matter" and "form" (as expounded in Aristotelean metaphysics, "baptized" by St. Thomas Aquinas, and defined by the Council of Florence in the 15th century)—namely, the right "stuff" (like bread, wine, blessed oil, blessed water), and the correct words. As long as the right words were said with the right stuff (or over the right people), the sacrament "worked"—it "took"—it was "valid," that is, it did not have to be repeated. Grace was guaranteed—since that is what *ex opere operato* was all about.

Based on the decades-old "Liturgical Movement," the liturgical studies that occurred in the 1900s, however, especially after the Second Vatican Council, have, at least on one level, changed many of these notions. Even in official documents and books, we see an emphasis on sign, symbol, and style. Contemporary authors describe sacraments in ways that might scandalize our ancestors, yet in words that are probably closer to the original sense of what was happening, at least as far as the first few generations of Christians were concerned. For example, the late American theologian Tad Guzie wrote:

> A sacrament is a festive action in which Christians assemble to celebrate their lived experience and to call to heart their common story. The action is a symbol of God's care for us in Christ. Enacting the symbol brings us closer to one another in the church and to the Lord who is there for us.[1]

In a similar way, Father David Power proposes this definition of liturgy:

> The liturgy is an action wherein the testimony of God is heard and appropriated, the experience of the community is transformed, and a godly presence disclosed.[2]

Even in official Roman documents, we see a dramatic shift in emphasis (sometimes inconsistently juxtaposed with older formulations) in the *Prænotanda* or *Introductions* to the revised liturgical rites. Take, for example, the comments on sign and symbol mentioned in the *General Instruction of the Roman Missal* (GIRM) concerning the bread to be used at Mass (#321) (emphasis added): "The *meaning of the sign demands* that the material for the Eucharistic celebration truly have the appearance of food."

And this excerpt is not a unique, isolated instance of this newer mindset, a mindset concerned with the authenticity of the signs used in liturgical celebrations. Perhaps a few other references would also be appropriate (emphasis added).

Introduction to the Lectionary #35: Along with the ministers, the actions, the allocated places, and other elements, the books containing the readings of the word of God remind the hearers of the presence of God speaking to his people. Since, in liturgical celebrations the books too serve as *signs and symbols* of the higher realities, care must be taken to ensure that they truly are worthy, dignified and beautiful.

GIRM #85: It is most desirable that the faithful, just as the priest himself is bound to do, receive the Lord's Body from hosts consecrated at the same Mass and that, in the instances when it is permitted, they partake of the chalice (cf. no. 283), so that *even by means of the signs* Communion will stand out more clearly as a participation in the sacrifice actually being celebrated.

GIRM #281: Holy Communion has a fuller form *as a sign* when it is distributed under both kinds. For in this form *the sign* of the Eucharistic banquet is more clearly evident and clear expression is given to the divine will by which the new and eternal Covenant is ratified in the Blood of the Lord.

Pastoral Care of the Sick (1983 English language edition) #107: If the anointing is to be an *effective sacramental symbol,* there should be a generous use of oil so that it will be seen and felt by the sick person *as a sign* of the Spirit's healing and strengthening presence. For the same reason, it is not desirable to wipe off the oil after the anointing.

Catechism of the Catholic Church (CCC) n. 1146: In human life, *signs and symbols* occupy an important place. As a being at once body and spirit, man expresses and perceives spiritual realities through physical *signs and symbols.* As a social being, man needs *signs and symbols* to communicate with others, through language, gestures, and actions. The same holds true for his relationship with God.

CCC n. 1152: The sacraments of the Church do not abolish but purify and integrate all the richness of the *signs and symbols* of the cosmos and of social life.

This resensitization to the role of symbol in liturgy needs to be taken to heart if we are really to continue to make the liturgy come alive in our contemporary world. Even after the forty years since the promulgation of the Second Vatican Council's *Constitution on the Liturgy,* we have not completely come to grips with the implications and thrust of the renewed liturgy. As one commentator wrote (paraphrasing G. K. Chesterton), it is not that the new liturgy has been tried and found wanting, it is that it has never really been tried.

A major problem with the distant past with regard to liturgy is that we had too many symbols, the majority of which had nothing really to do with what was important. The problem that exists in the recent past and the present is that we reacted too violently against that heritage, have thrown out *all* symbols, and have resorted to words to such an extent that our liturgies become an avalanche of words and we still ignore the primary symbols. And this avalanche of words is, upon closer analysis, merely a reworking of the worst of an older liturgical theology.

The misuse of symbols and signs is also related to a spirit of efficiency, convenience, and minimalism that pervades the American way of life. McDonald's restaurants, and personal computers, are, for some people, the paradigms for good liturgies and good liturgical practice. But people are not machines, and what may be tolerable as an occasional convenience in a busy world can become significantly detrimental in the world of divine life and love.

Perhaps this idea is better expressed in the following quote from an issue of the Canadian *National Bulletin on Liturgy* (emphasis added):

> The Church uses symbols in celebrating the liturgy. It is *not the material element alone, but our use of it that is symbolic:* we use water in the baptismal bath, bread and wine in the eucharistic meal, oil in the anointing of the body in various rites. If *we use the symbol generously,* we are reflecting God's generous gifts to us in Christ. If we are miserly, using the minimum of gestures and actions, we prevent others from seeing and feeling the fullness of God's love. A Church that limits itself to *minimalism will be stunted in its faith and liturgy* and growth in love.[3]

Because our communal worship is centered on symbol, it cannot be overemphasized how important it is to use the important symbols well, and not let them be overwhelmed by what is relatively minor. Using symbols well will lead to a better total celebration. There is still too much of the old mentality of "just so long as the right words are said, that is really all that is necessary." Too many of us learned the meaning of *ex opere operato* too well in the days before Vatican II, and even after over thirty five years, we cannot put that mindset into a secondary position. Clinical studies indicate that only about 20% of human communication is verbal—the other 80% is non-verbal. It is important to use symbol well, for that is the way that most communication takes place during our celebrations. Unfortunately, we approach liturgy the same as we approach so many other things in our cerebral, technological world—with a rationalism that causes love to wane and the heart to wither. It is this approach that has worked against a better liturgy in our contemporary world. Father David Power remarks that

> it is worth reflecting on [the contemporary symbol crises], in order to perceive the better what issues are at stake in the renewal of liturgy as a symbol system, and also perhaps to understand why too cerebral and organizational an approach to liturgical change has not borne the fruits apparently intended.[4]

The document *Environment and Art in Catholic Worship,* issued in 1978 by the U.S. Bishops' Committee on the Liturgy, devoted two paragraphs to the topic of "Opening Up of Symbols," and it is worthwhile to recall what this document says, particularly since it brings up the question of liturgical minimalism.

> 14. Every word, gesture, movement, object, appointment must be real in the sense that it is our own. It must come from the deepest understanding of ourselves (not careless, phony, counterfeit, pretentious, exaggerated, etc.). Liturgy has suffered historically from a kind of minimalism and an overriding concern for efficiency, partly because sacramental causality and efficacy have been emphasized at the expense of sacramental signification. As our symbols tended in practice to shrivel up and petrify, they became much more manageable and efficient. They still 'caused,' were still 'efficacious' even though they had often ceased to signify in the richest, fullest sense.

> 15. Renewal requires the opening up of our symbols, especially the fundamental ones of bread and wine, water, oil, the laying on of hands, until we can experience all of them as authentic and appreciate their symbolic value.

In November 2000, the U.S. bishops approved a successor document to *Environment and Art* entitled *Built of Living Stones*. Although this newer document is geared more toward practical issues involved in the construction or renovation of churches, it nevertheless continues to include references to fundamental liturgical principles. For example, we read the following:

> 26. Poorly utilized or minimal signs do not enliven the community's faith and can even diminish active participation.* It must likewise be kept in mind that the liturgy and its signs and symbols do not exercise merely a teaching function. They also touch and move a person to conversion of heart and not simply to enlightenment of mind.
>
> *Cf. National Conference of Catholic Bishops' Committee on the Liturgy, *Music in Catholic Worship* [MCW] 1983, Nos. 6–7.

The Canadian *National Bulletin on Liturgy* also reminds us of the importance of the symbolic in our lives over and above the merely legal:

> The quality of celebration has a strong effect on all who take part. Celebrations which are weak, slovenly, hasty, verbose, unprepared, or indifferent will weaken the faith of all present. Celebrations which are strong, joyful, carefully prepared, and well celebrated will help to deepen the faith and love of the participants. Good celebrations are a sign of our faith, and can strengthen it in all who share in the event.[5]

These same ideas were stated in slightly different words in another statement issued by the U.S. Bishops' Committee on the Liturgy, entitled *Music in Catholic Worship* (emphasis added):

4. People in love make signs of love, not only to express their love but also to deepen it. Love never expressed dies. Christians' love for Christ and for one another and Christians' faith in Christ and in one another must be expressed *in the signs and symbols of celebration* or they will die.

6. Faith grows when it is well expressed in celebration. Good celebrations foster and nourish faith. Poor celebrations may weaken and destroy it.[6]

The criteria we use to determine whether a given celebration was "good" can no longer be reduced to merely checking whether the rubrics had been exactly followed. One reason for this is that the present rubrics do not exactly determine actions and options now as they did in the Tridentine Missal. Many times the rubrics specify multiple options. (For example, look at the following rubric from the Latin edition of the *Rite of Anointing the Sick*, #73: "the following litany may be said here, or after the anointing, or even, according to circumstances, at some other point. The priest may adapt or shorten the text." One would be hard pressed to find a more liberal rubric anywhere!) At other times, the rubrics give underlying principles and leave the exact execution to the sensibilities of the one who presides. (For example, in the *Rite of Penance* we read in #41: "When the penitent comes to confess his sins, the priest welcomes him warmly and greets him with kindness.") Thus, in our contemporary world, our contemporary liturgies must be judged by contemporary standards based on contemporary insights into the nature of liturgy, of sacred symbol, and of the human longing for divine love.

This book is an attempt to open eyes to some of the contemporary insights and contemporary standards. The attempt is by way of the *via negativa,* the method of counterexamples. It is a method that has been used for centuries both in theology and science, especially physics and mathematics. One learns about a concept through looking at what a concept should NOT be. We cannot really say, positively, much about God, for example. But we can affirm what God is NOT. It is hoped that the negative rules, examples, and principles given throughout this book may give rise to positive results—to a positive appreciation of what the revised vision of the liturgy is really about, to a positive appreciation of what should be absent and present in good liturgy, to a positive appreciation of how Tridentine practices still creep into our liturgies to the detriment of the sacramental experience for post-Vatican II Christians.

But does this negative approach lead to a depressing outlook? Not necessarily. In fact, this negative-to-positive approach even has scriptural foundations. The majority of the Ten Commandments are phrased negatively—but they form the basis of a very positive covenant with God. In Luke's version of the Beatitudes (Luke 6:20–26), the four (positive) beatitudes are matched with four (negative) woes. Together, they describe a balanced pattern of life for a follower of the Lord. On the other hand, Christ's warning to the Pharisees was all negative in Matthew's Gospel (23:13–36). Yet, this is interpreted as positive teaching for Christ's followers.

Some might accuse me of being "nitpicky," of making liturgical mountains out of rubrical molehills. It is true that all rubrics are not of equal importance. In the *Decree on Ecumenism* of the Second Vatican Council, we are told that "in Catholic doctrine, there exists an order or 'hierarchy' of truths" (Cpt 2, #11), and the same principle also holds in liturgy—some things are more important than others. Too often, however, the impression is given at certain liturgies that everything is of equally little value. Details are important—attention to detail is what makes a good performance, whether it be a play, a symphony, or a dinner. The late Father Robert Hovda, formerly of the Liturgical Conference, writing about details and the liturgy,[7] quotes the words of William Blake which seem very apropos: "He who would do good to others must do it in minute particulars; 'General Good' is the plea of the scoundrel, hypocrite & flatterer. For art & science cannot exist but in minutely organized particulars, And not in generalizing demonstrations of the rational power." There are too many liturgies which are being evaluated as "generally good," but upon closer examination (of the "minutely organized particulars"), leave much to be desired. Like a good recipe, the minute details of the spices help bring out the flavor of the main entree—the spices should not drown out the main entree, but help us appreciate it. The same holds true for liturgy.

It may also seem that this book is overly concerned with liturgical law and the many rubrics that exist, and not really concerned about the underlying spirit. In one sense, it is correct that rubrics are emphasized in the sections that follow, but only because I believe that law tries to enflesh more important underlying principles and less important cultural options for the purpose of preserving the heritage within a given tradition and in a cultural manner with which most people would feel comfortable. But law is only one aspect of what liturgy totally is. Liturgy also involves culture, theology, psychology, history, to name a few other "supporting" disciplines. We can break a law and at the same time be on very good grounds theologically, psychologically, symbolically, historically, and culturally. But, in my experience, that occurs rarely. More often, when rubrics are violated, other aspects of the liturgical experience are damaged as well, and this book is concerned with the total experience—an experience that should help lead people to a deeper love and praise of their God. In some situations, a law can be good—eliminating bad liturgical practices, like the law stating that there should be no music during the eucharistic prayer.[8] We do not need competition during the most important prayer of the Mass. The same law, however, can be enforced counterliturgically, as when an instrument is needed to help a presiding priest sing the eucharistic prayer and the assembly sing their acclamations. In cases like these, we do well to respectfully "violate" an unliturgical interpretation of the law, without violating its fundamental purpose and spirit. My intent is to help the reader to learn the true spirit of what may seem to be very confusing (and at times antiliturgical) rubrics and liturgical laws. We need always remember that just because something is legal does not make it morally right or personally expedient—for example, the legality of brothels in Nevada or of abortions in the United States. Similarly, just because something is illegal does not make it morally evil: it is legal for the Byzantine Rite to use leavened bread at the Eucharist, but not for the Roman Rite. Law is more complicated than we tend, at times, to admit. Law is also less absolute than we tend, at times, to practice.[9]

Although the suggestions that follow are given as absolutes, very little is really absolute in this world. The wording is occasionally strong to indicate the importance that many liturgists attach to the topic under discussion, but some of the practices may allow for variation in special circumstances. When the *special* becomes the *typical,* however, it is then that the general thrust of good liturgy may (quite possibly) be ignored, and it is then that the liturgical experience of the assembly will suffer.

NOTES

1. Guzie, *The Book of Sacramental Basics,* p. 53.

2. Power, *Unsearchable Riches,* p. 146.

3. Canadian *National Bulletin on Liturgy,* v. 16, #91 (Nov.–Dec. 1983), p. 215.

4. Power, *Unsearchable Riches,* p. 10.

5. Canadian *Bulletin,* v. 16, #91 (Nov.–Dec. 1983), p. 221.

6. *Music in Catholic Worship,* First Edition 1972, Second Edition 1983.

7. Hovda, "It Begins With The Assembly," in *A Reader: The Environment for Worship,* p. 41, quoting William Blake, "Jerusalem, Emanation of the Giant Albion," Ch. 3, plate 55, lines 60–63.

8. Cf. *Inæstimabile Donum* #6; GIRM #32, cf. DOL-1402 and footnote R1; GIRM #78.

9. The *Code of Canon Law* ends with the reminder, "...the salvation of souls...is always the supreme law of the Church" (can. 1752).

SOME THOUGHTS ON SYMBOLS

Reverence symbols in all areas of life.

Symbols exist everywhere, but they reach a certain apex in our spiritual life in their presence in the eucharistic celebration. It is a highly symbolic gesture when a husband gives his wife a rose. But if the rose is given every year on their wedding anniversary, much more is conveyed than the presence of a simple rose. So it is with the Eucharist—it makes more sense when we see it in context with the other symbols in our religious lives and see religious symbols in context with symbols in nonreligious aspects of our lives. As Father David Power says:

> Liturgy is not the sole symbolic reality, but it belongs alongside the scriptures and other manifestations such as icons. It is distinct from these not in being symbolic but in being the gathering and celebration of the body, the place where the church assumes its full form, bringing into a common expression of faith and joy all the other symbols that belong in this mystery.[1]

To reiterate, sometimes we tend to overlook significant symbols in our lives, much to the detriment of interpersonal relationships. People of other cultures interpret gestures much more symbolically and can be offended when individuals from a technologically oriented society, for example, take a pragmatic attitude toward certain actions and things. Let me give you two significant examples, both of which occurred several years ago.

In November, 1979, Pope John Paul II traveled to Istanbul, Turkey to meet with the late Orthodox Patriarch Dimitrios I. Gifts were exchanged—but most people overlooked the great symbolism attached to those gifts.[2] The pope gave the patriarch a replica of one of the most famous icons of the Roman Church, a copy of the icon of Our Lady of Czestochowa. This symbolized the Roman Church's devotion to the Mother of God and reverence of iconography, a "sacramental" in Orthodoxy. The patriarch gave the pope an omophorion (the Byzantine equivalent of the pallium), which is used by all Byzantine Rite bishops as a sign of their authority. This symbolized that Orthodoxy recognized the episcopacy and episcopal authority of the pope, even though they do not agree with his universal jurisdiction. More than being mere trinkets, these two gifts were signs of willingness to acknowledge the truth of each church's positions on significant issues.

After Pope John Paul II was shot on May 13, 1981, he left his recovery bed to speak briefly at a meeting between Orthodox and Catholics held in St. Peter's on Pentecost. He mentioned the writings of "Saint" Gregory Palamas, a theologian who died after the formal break between East and West in 1054. Gregory is held in high esteem among the Orthodox and his feast is celebrated on the Second Sunday of Lent. His feast, however, has never been celebrated in the West and among Eastern Christians in union with Rome. In addition, he was never officially canonized by the Roman Church because of questionable theology. Nevertheless, the pope referred to him as "Saint" Gregory, another extremely symbolic gesture which probably did more to heal the division between East and West than a whole series of theological discussions.

Symbols are extremely important in life. Yet we too often overlook them or ignore them, because they are not as explicit and practical as we might want them to be. We need to be less practical and more reverential when we approach the symbols of liturgy.

Remember that the basic symbol of the Eucharist is one bread and one cup.

If we do not pay attention to the central elements of the Eucharist, we are missing the boat. If these elements are obscured, something is wrong. If the fullness of the central symbols are withheld from the assembly (e.g., no Communion from the chalice), the result is an impoverished liturgical experience.

Oneness is important, and newer legislation insists that only one vessel of bread and one chalice should be used during the eucharistic prayer, until the breaking of the bread (see section 7). Symbolically, this practice emphasizes one of the "fruits" of the Mass—the unity of the community.

In addition, the bread should look like bread, and even the Roman Missal demands this authenticity of sign (cf. GIRM #321), but homebaked bread is not an absolute value over the fundamental sign of one bread and one cup. It is humorous to see homebaked little "hosts," or to see homebaked bread precut into small sections before the liturgy begins. Granted it is necessary to have enough elements, yet not over consecrate, but one should not value such practices at the expense of a more basic symbol of the liturgy!

Oneness also means that, when using hosts, the distinction between a "priest's host" and the "people's hosts" should be eliminated as much as possible. The GIRM notes that "it is...expedient that the Eucharistic bread...be made in such a way that the priest at Mass with a congregation is able in practice to break it into parts for distribution to at least some of the faithful" (#321). As a result, the practice associated with the Tridentine Missal, in which the priest consumed all of the "priest's host," should be avoided. Whenever possible, larger-sized hosts (e.g., 5–6" in diameter) should be used and broken into numerous particles from which both priest and people partake. At smaller Masses, such as on weekdays, it may even be possible to use several larger-sized hosts, to be broken for all communicants present, thus completely eliminating the need to use individual small hosts for the assembly.

Do not do damage to strong liturgical symbols through unnecessary clutter.

One basic liturgical principle is recognizing major symbols and enhancing them. But enhancing something in a liturgical context frequently means permitting the symbols to stand on their own rather than drown them in clutter. Architecturally, the focal points of liturgy in a church are the altar (a symbol of Christ in the Book of Revelation, cf. GIRM #298), the font, the ambo, the chair. To make one piece of furniture compete with the others, or to clutter the furniture in such a way that one wonders what is what (e.g., to turn the altar into the cave of Bethlehem at Christmas[3]) is far from being good liturgical practice.

The ideal of the GIRM is that only those items required for Mass should be on the altar and then only when needed (cf. GIRM #306). Thus, the altar initially should have *nothing* on it (including candles—they are better placed around the altar than on it[4]). After the entrance procession, the Book of the Gospels, if used, should be the only item present on the altar. Then, after the procession with the gifts, ideally there should be only one cup and one loaf (cf. 1 Cor 10) on the altar—nothing more should be visible (the missal is tolerated, but among the Russian Byzantines, even the priest's liturgical book is not allowed on the altar!). (See section 7 for comments on what to do if more bread and wine is needed for the Communion of the assembly than can be contained in a single vessel and single chalice.) To put cruets and a finger bowl also on the altar when movable credence tables can be discreetly located nearby should be considered a crime against good liturgy. To have the chalice on the altar from the beginning of the Mass should be considered far less than ideal. A presiding priest should not make the altar into the pastor's desk, similar to the presidential desk used for speeches to the nation. If you are the president, it may be appropriate to have microphones visible, along with pictures of the wife and kids, a pen and pencil set, reading glasses, speech notes, and so forth, on the desk top, but the altar is not a desk and it should be reserved for the symbols of Christ alone— one vessel of bread, one chalice, the Book of the Gospels (and, in contemporary society, to aid the memory of the priest, the missal—although this was not needed in the early church). Thus, a modern presider should take care to remove missalettes, reading glasses, homily notes, ugly microphones, and the like, from the table of the Lord!

Do not distract from the praise of God with unexpected symbolic clashes!

Psalm 150 suggests that we praise God with "clashing cymbals," but more often than not, clashing *symbols* detract from the praise of God rather than adding to it.

I was startled by a conversation I had a number of years ago with a professor of communication who is fairly well respected in his field. He told me how jarring it was for him to watch one of the televised Masses of Pope John Paul II. The point of irritation was the fairly modern watch the pope was wearing which was quite visible whenever closeups of the pope were shown.

My acquaintance, who over the years had become sensitive to subliminal forms of communication, body language, and the power of symbols, said that he was very much struck by the pope, as a symbol of the permanence of Christianity, celebrating the Eucharist, a symbol of an eternal God's infinite love for the human race, with this blaring symbol of a modern, time-conscious culture. Instead of being drawn beyond the limits of this world, my friend felt himself being pulled into the worst aspects of the present speed-conscious culture.

This is just one example of symbolic clashes which can and do occur during the liturgy. Few such clashes, if any, help the community's prayer life. Thus, we must constantly be sensitive to such possible clashes and eliminate them as much as possible.

Do not underestimate the subconscious power of symbols.

Robert Burns, in his poem "To a Mouse," has given us words appropriate for many human situations:

The best-laid schemes o' mice an' men
Gang aft a-gley.

No matter how hard we plan, our schemes "gang aft a-gley," that is, often do go awry. One of the greatest planning disasters in recent history in the United States was the introduction of the Susan B. Anthony dollar coin in 1979. The reasons given for its introduction were, for the most part, well thought out and promising. The project, however, was an abysmal failure. Many would attribute its failure to an unspoken, symbolic problem: "How can this coin be a dollar when it looks like a quarter? It's un-American to have a dollar that small! A dollar should be a paper bill or big enough to put into a Nevada slot machine."

On the rational, cerebral level, the Susan B. Anthony dollar was a money-saving answer to a great problem—the rapid wearing-out of paper dollar bills. But none of the planners realized the symbolic problems that it would raise and the possible failure of the plan due to these nonrational, nonpractical, yet very real symbolic concerns. The Sacajawea dollar coin, issued in 2000, is having a better reception, probably due to its gold-colored hue, giving it a distinctiveness and "richness" the Anthony dollar didn't seem to have.

I would suggest that we frequently do similar things in liturgies. Our cerebral plans may seem to "work," but on the symbolic level they are disasters, since they do not perdure nor do they increase the faith commitment of members of the community. We too easily tend to dismiss the more important symbols of our liturgy—baptism by immersion, Communion under both kinds—as being impractical. But the Anthony dollar coin was meant to be practical and it still did not work! Practicality can be an enemy of good liturgy, if it overwhelms a fundamental symbol, disguises it, or reduces it to a bare minimum. We need to identify the basic symbols of our liturgy, enhance them (without worrying about efficiency or practicality), experience the fullness of these symbols, and only then plan about the secondary aspects of the rites. If we let our fundamental symbols speak for themselves to the fullest extent possible, we may learn that other parts of the liturgy are much easier to plan, and we may avoid Susan B. Anthony-type liturgical disasters.

NOTES

1. Power, *Unsearchable Riches,* p. 47.

2. Cf. *Origins,* v. 9 (Nov. 1979), p. 421.

3. Cf. *Built of Living Stones,* n. 124. Also see *Book of Blessings* (U.S. edition), n. 1544.

4. Cf. *Built of Living Stones,* n. 92.

SOME THOUGHTS ON PRESIDING

Presiders should preside.

Presiding is a developed art form, akin to being a good orchestra conductor. Priests, and others who, because of a lack of priests lead a community in prayer, need to know how to delegate, because being a presider differs from being a factotum. Those who preside also need to know when and how to exercise leadership, yet allow their leadership to reflect the awe of the mystery of communicating with the divine.

Some individuals who preside have a stained glass window kind of voice which projects timidity rather than strength. Others seem to hide in the background in the name of "baptismal equality" and "democracy." One should not negate the theological truth that (in one sense) we are all equal through our common baptism, and that democracy has a role even in a hierarchical church structure. Nevertheless, the liturgy needs leadership in the same way that an orchestra needs a conductor. Therefore, one of the continuing tasks of priests and other leaders of prayer is to learn how to preside better, so that they might better serve the assembled people of God.

For a number of years, the Davies Symphony Hall in San Francisco has been sold out for the pre-Christmas sing-along performances of Handel's *Messiah*. This is a beautiful "secular" parallel of what good liturgy and presiding should be about. The conductor (= presiding priest) is a must! The musicians (= ministers of the word, of music, of the Eucharist) are also a must! The audience (= assembly) is also a must if this is to be the experience that everyone present hopes it will be. The conductor (= presiding priest) does not do everything by himself, but his services are necessary. Unfortunately for the analogy, the orchestra conductor usually doesn't sing or play the major solo as a presiding priest must do during the liturgy (i.e., the eucharistic prayer), but this parallel does bring out how a good liturgy is a coordination of efforts.

Do not underplay the role of the presider.

The late Father Robert Hovda suggested that the presiding priest has five major tasks to perform in the liturgy.[1]

1. *Directing the entire service* while leaving to other ministers other roles. The one who presides must graciously coordinate ministries while still remaining "in charge" of the entire worship service.

2. *Defining the beginning and end of the entire service.*

3. *Leading prayer, in particular the eucharistic prayer.* In the Roman tradition, the presiding priest formulates and voices five prayers in the course of the liturgy: (a) the collect (opening prayer), (b) the prayer concluding the prayer of the faithful, (c) the prayer over the offerings, (d) the eucharistic prayer, and (e) the prayer after Communion. The eucharistic prayer is, of course, the high point of the presiding priest's public praying, but not the only prayer he speaks. Note that this duty of leading prayer also demands that other prayers (such as the prayer concluding the prayer of the faithful) not be delegated to others either.

4. *Distributing Communion with his own hand.* A point made by the late Father Godfrey Diekmann, O.S.B., in his research into historical texts is that a key role of the presiding priest is to distribute Communion from the elements that he consecrated, an action which is intimately connected with proclaiming the eucharistic

prayer. Therefore, one must question the practice of letting others exclusively do the work of distributing Communion on the (shaky) basis that "all the priest has to do is say the words of consecration." One also has to question the practice, often seen years ago when bishops celebrated, of letting priests distribute Communion, while the bishop rested at the chair.

5. *Proclaiming the word.* Giving the homily is a normal task for the presiding priest, although it may happen that it is delegated to another, for example, to a concelebrant or a deacon. (As will be noted in section 6, however, "proclaiming the word" does not mean that the presiding priest must himself read the Scripture during the liturgy.)

Do not overplay the role of the presider.

A reoccurring theme in various documents is that during the liturgy "all,…whether they are ordained ministers or lay Christian faithful,…should carry out solely but completely that which pertains to them."[2] Those who preside, whether they are ordained or lay, should not usurp the functions of any other minister, nor should they over-delegate presidential functions to others. In planning the liturgy, a presiding priest needs to solicit advice from his coworkers, yet, since he is ultimately the sole one who presides, he should not let others make all decisions pertaining to his role.[3]

The presiding priest should never look like a reluctant sorcerer dragged in to say the magic words at the right time while others are "really" running the "show." Liturgy, like an orchestral performance, is a coordination of efforts, prayers, talents, and deferences so that the end result is that God is praised, rather than the ministers receiving pats on their backs.

Do not forget about the congregation.

The liturgy is not something the presiding priest does FOR the people. Rather, it is something the assembled group of Christians, whose gifts are coordinated by a presider, does TOGETHER. *Environment and Art* reminds us of this truth:

> Among the symbols with which liturgy deals, none is more important than this assembly of believers....The most powerful experience of the sacred is found in the celebration and the persons celebrating, that is, it is found in the action of the assembly: the living words, the living gestures, the living sacrifice, the living meal. This was at the heart of the earliest liturgies.[4]

Built of Living Stones also proclaims the same message:

> ...in the liturgical assembly, there is no audience. Rather, the entire congregation acts.[5]

Never merely "say Mass!"

Gone are the days when all a priest had to do was "say Mass." This mentality lingers, however, and negatively infects many a eucharistic gathering. The priest who presides must exercise a position of loving, serving leadership in the assembly of the baptized, but can never totally substitute for the assembly and should never usurp ministries that properly belong to others. Therefore, it is wrong for any priest who presides always to proclaim all the readings himself, if there are competent lectors in the assembly. It is wrong for the one who presides to ignore the legitimate demands of the assembly. It is wrong for a presider to preside as if the assembly were merely frosting on the cake, and not the meat of the meal.

Do not usurp another's proper part.

More than one leader of prayer has the bad habit of saying "Amen" when this should not be done, for example, as the conclusion to the initial sign of the cross. By so doing, the one who presides is usurping a response which properly belongs to the assembly and depriving them of active participation in the liturgical action at that point. This practice can have detrimental effects in other places. If enough presiders do this sort of thing often enough, the reverse of the Pavlov's dog syndrome can be induced. As a result, instead of always responding when given the cue, the assembly may be lulled into non-response.

Do not forget that the one who presides is a public figure in a quasi-dramatic setting. Thus, special attention needs to be given to what others see and what they should hear.

Because the one who presides is a public figure, things that might perhaps be tolerable in private become rude and offensive in the liturgical context. Because the liturgy is, in effect, a quasi-dramatic setting using stylized movements, "choreography," and a "script," many of the common-sense guidelines for actors are also applicable to all the ministers of the liturgy.

For example, all ministers should vest with care. Dangling ends of cinctures should never be permitted.

When speaking to the assembly, ministers should keep proper eye contact with the assembly. Few things are as counter-symbolic as a presiding priest (or a deacon who proclaims the Gospel) who looks at the book while saying, "The Lord be with you!"

When speaking to the people, ministers should make sure they are heard, gently ignoring, if need be, the microphone system. Wireless microphones often need special attention (i.e., which direction to toggle the on/off switch to turn the mike on), especially by visiting priests. Too often, ministers assume that since there is a microphone in front of them, they do not have to speak loudly, project, or speak directly into the microphone. Some microphones are "directional" and will not pick up any sound that is not spoken directly into the tip. Unfortunately, in front of a microphone some ministers even tone down their voice to merely a whisper. In many situations, doing so can be disastrous. Most PA systems are set so that only a normal speaking voice is amplified properly and frequently church PA systems leave a lot to be desired. As a result, in some churches, priests and other ministers might need to fight against the electronic "helps" to make themselves heard by the assembly!

Those who have oversight of a community should also reflect on visibility and audibility issues for all in the assembly. For example, in a community where there are large numbers of older individuals, there may be need for special earphones in the pews for any hearing-impaired members in the assembly in order to enable all to participate actively and fully.

Do not do damage to the shape and flow of the liturgy.

Many presiding priests preside as if the liturgy were a disparate juxtaposition of nonrelated rites. Most scholars would agree that the various parts of the liturgy are all interconnected, but it requires special concentration for the one presiding to convey the interconnection to the assembly. Too often, some presiding ministers seem not to be aware of the flow of the liturgy and even seem to be building dams to stop the flow at

various points. Such presiders need to be encouraged to take
time to reacquaint themselves with the liturgy, its unity, its various parts, and their interconnections.

Do not make gestures as if you were a robot.

The gestures of the liturgy are human gestures, even though
they are somewhat stylized, dramatic gestures. The mentality of
the pre-Vatican II liturgy forced presiding priests to perform the
major gestures as if they were robots performing strange magical rites and, unfortunately, some presiders whose formation
took place before 1965 still cling to this style (albeit perhaps
unconsciously). Even some who have been ordained since
Vatican II have learned more from the visual example of older
priests than from studying the text of the rubrics and reflecting
on the meaning of various gestures.

There are four major hand and arm gestures used by priests
during liturgies and these gestures invite a few comments to
clarify how they are done, as well as when they are to be used.[6]

JOINED HANDS are used whenever the one presiding
addresses the assembly, for example, when saying "let us pray"
before the collect (opening prayer), or when introducing the
prayer of the faithful.

EXTENDED ("Greeting") HANDS are used by priests when
GREETING the assembly, for example, when saying "The Lord be
with you." This should be seen as a human gesture imitating the
gesture one would make right before embracing a friend.

EXTENDED ("Praying") HANDS are used by priests when
praying the public presidential prayers. This *orans* gesture is
NOT used for private prayers (e.g., the priestly prayers before
Communion), and it is also NOT used for introductions to
prayers which are addressed to the assembly (e.g., "Let us
pray"). This gesture should also be seen as a human gesture of

reaching out to heaven, with palms almost straight up, hands about head high, arms about halfway between being straight out from the side and straight ahead.

EXTENDED ("Imposition") HANDS are used in blessings and gestures of sanctification. This is a stylized variant of the human gesture of a gentle touch. This gesture is used especially at ordination, but also in reconciling sinners, in anointing the sick, and at confirmation. During the Eucharist, this is the gesture made over the offerings during the epicletic section of the eucharistic prayer, and also over the assembly during a solemn blessing or prayer over the people.

Beware of omitting gesture.

Prior to the Second Vatican Council, one of the items of standard equipment that every religious sister possessed when teaching grammar school was the clicker—that little device that resembled flat castanets and was used primarily to make a distinct sound. This sound was the key used to indicate when to stand or kneel or genuflect when in church.

After the Council, many Catholics reacted to this regimentation and, especially in small group Masses, unconsciously decided that "enlightened" Catholics have grown beyond gesture (and bodily postures). We are a body-people, however. We communicate bodily, not via ESP. In the secular world we follow certain conventions, like standing when giving standing ovations, or when dignitaries enter a room. The church has used these human conventions for centuries for the same basic reasons—they enable us bodily to express our belief in the importance of things or persons (standing or genuflecting), or to express unity (sitting or standing), or to express feelings (striking the breast or kneeling).

Gestures are important both for the assembly and for the one who presides. *Environment and Art* reminds us of the following:

> The liturgy of the Church has been rich in a tradition of ritual movement and gestures. These actions, subtly, yet really, contribute to an environment which can foster prayer or which can distract from prayer. When the gestures are done in common, they contribute to the unity of the worshiping assembly. Gestures which are broad and full in both a visual and tactile sense, support the entire symbolic ritual. When the gestures are done by the presiding minister, they can either engage the entire assembly and bring them into an even greater unity, or if done poorly, they can isolate.[7]

Built of Living Stones offers similar advice:

> Gestures, language, and actions are the *physical, visible,* and *public* expressions by which human beings understand and manifest their inner life. Since human beings on this earth are always made of flesh and blood, they not only will and think, but also speak and sing, move and celebrate. These human actions as well as physical objects are also the signs by which Christians express and deepen their relationship to God.[8]

We must not lightly dispense with posture changes, for example. It may be awkward in a small liturgy to stand for the Gospel or to stand for the eucharistic prayer, but perhaps the awkwardness will just emphasize the importance of the given parts even more. It may seem like a minor thing to omit the sign of the cross at the beginning of the liturgy, or the crosses before the Gospel, or kissing the Book of the Gospels, but these gestures help engage each Christian present, and reiterate the truth that we do not worship God with our minds alone, but with "all our heart, all our soul, and all our strength" (Deut 6:5).

Do not sing unless you can!

One should not abandon all hope of singing if one is not a Caruso or a Pavarotti, but one of the greatest crosses in the pre-Vatican II church was having to endure the cacophonous warblings of an aging pastor who could not carry a tune in a bucket. Since nothing is absolutely required to be sung by a presiding priest by the present missal, the priest doesn't have to worry about his inability to sing. Thus, a priest need not inflict his lack of talent on an assembly. On the other hand, singing can greatly enhance a liturgy, if it is done with at least a minimal amount of competence. If a presiding priest with an ordinary singing voice sings at least the preface and doxology of the eucharistic prayer, it can be a great encouragement to many in the assembly, also possessing ordinary voices, to sing their praise of God as well, and thus lead to a better overall liturgical experience for all present.

Do not neglect to prepare the physical implements.

In particular, prepare the missal. Do not flip through the pages of the altar missal while the assembly is responding. This is both rude, impolite, and might even be considered a sin against good liturgy.

Never perform two (visible) actions at the same time.

Trying to do two things at the same time can be one of the natural results of not preparing well. Some presiding priests must find the correct collect in the missal while the assembly is praying the Gloria. Others are counting out hosts into the ciborium while the assembly is proclaiming the Creed. If this type of behavior were done by actors in a play, the play would not last past opening night!

NOTES

1. Hovda, *Strong, Loving and Wise,* pp. 36, 40.
2. GIRM #91; *Constitution on the Liturgy* #28, DOL-28.
3. GIRM ##352, 111.
4. *Environment and Art* ##28–29.
5. *Built of Living Stones* #51.
6. Roman liturgical books make a distinction between gestures by bishops and priests, and gestures by deacons and lay presiders. For example, before the Gospel, a deacon (or priest if there is no deacon) does *not* extend his hands for the greeting (GIRM ##175, 134). Lay presiders do not use extended hands when saying public prayers (e.g., *Book of Blessings* [U.S. edition], n. 57). Also, in previous editions of the missals, prayers of blessing were said with hands *joined* (e.g., blessing of ashes, palms, candles, water). In the 2002 edition of the missal, such prayers are now said with hands *extended* (the one exception is for the blessing of water in lieu of the act of penitence, but this may be a typographical error since for every other such prayer of blessing, the hand gesture has been changed).
7. *Environment and Art* #56.
8. *Built of Living Stones* #24.

SOME GENERAL LITURGICAL PRINCIPLES

Do not take liturgical law too seriously nor too lightly.

The rubrics and other laws which describe and govern liturgy are *human* laws and, for the most part, can be modified in years ahead. Yet, they are an attempt to describe patterns of human behavior in a given formal situation (e.g., a eucharistic liturgy) based on tradition, theology, culture, the nature of symbol, the demands of the Gospel, and the needs of the community.

As mentioned at the end of section 1, a given liturgical law can sometimes eliminate a bad liturgical practice, but, in other situations, can be invoked in such a way as to stifle the development of good liturgy. The *law must be respected* because it offers us the wisdom of the ages and a method of incarnating liturgical principles into human actions. But the *law is not an end in itself*—only God's holy people, united by the Spirit in praising the Father of Jesus are such an end.

Never be comfortable with shoddy worship.

The biblical story of Cain and Abel can be interpreted as a story about authentic versus shoddy worship. Abel presented the best to God—thus his sacrifice of praise was accepted. Cain was comfortable with second best—his sacrifice was not accepted. How often in our eucharistic gatherings are we comfortable with second best, or even worse?

Do not make too much/too little out of the Mass.

The *Constitution on the Liturgy* tells us: "The liturgy is the summit toward which the activity of the Church is directed; at the same time it is the fountain from which all her power flows."[1] Yet, we are also told: "The sacred liturgy does not exhaust the entire activity of the Church. Before individuals can come to the liturgy they must be called to faith and to conversion."[2] And "the liturgy" is NOT synonymous with "the Eucharist." The eucharistic liturgy is the summit of the entire liturgical life, and the liturgy (in general) is the summit of all church activity. Church activity, however, should not be identified with the Eucharist alone. Yet, in the Roman Catholic tradition, there is a bad habit of being "over-Eucharistized" to the detriment of other prayer forms. Home Masses have been conducted at the drop of a hat and for relatively insignificant reasons, yet it is rare to find a parish that celebrates any part of the Liturgy of the Hours. The Eucharist as summit of the liturgy makes sense only if there exist other forms of liturgy. And the liturgy as summit of the church's activity makes sense only if there exist other forms of church activity.

Do not substitute/emphasize minor parts/actions in lieu of major ones.

The late Father Robert Hovda gave a very good example of this type of problem:

If, for example, in planning a eucharistic celebration, a group brings in a combo of musicians for song support, a batch of slides to help create an environment, a troupe of mime or dance specialists to illustrate the reading of the gospel, and does nothing about the bread and wine, it would not be unreasonable to send them all to bed without their suppers....But, because we are accustomed to a symbolic minimalism with respect to all sacraments, we tend to think that we have to bring in all sorts of entirely new elements to save this wretched rite....If we attended to the bread and wine, we would discover that the rite is powerful indeed.[3]

Even so-called "liturgical" helps can be relatively unliturgical. Hovda also wrote: "A booklet on the celebration of baptism came to this author's desk a few years ago: it was full of suggestions about peripheral aspects of the celebration; it said nothing at all about the actual bathing, the washing with water."[4]

In *Music in Catholic Worship,*[5] we find a good evaluation of which parts of the eucharistic liturgical rite are primary and which are secondary. When secondary rites overshadow what is primary, we are left with bad liturgy. For example, the second half of the Eucharist is shaped by the four verbs mentioned again and again in the New Testament at Last Supper accounts, at the multiplications of the loaves and fishes, and in the Emmaus account—*taking, blessing, breaking,* and *giving* (cf. GIRM #72). If a presiding priest performs the actions of the Mass so that the *breaking* of the bread is overshadowed by the kiss of peace or by the commingling of the bread and the wine, or the *taking* of the bread and wine is overshadowed by the washing of hands, or the *breaking* of the bread is telescoped into the prayer of blessing, the result is an impoverished liturgical experience for all present.

Do not misunderstand the positive qualities of the Roman liturgical tradition!

English liturgist Edmund Bishop (1846–1917) wrote: "The genius of the native Roman Rite is marked by simplicity, practicality, a great sobriety and self-control, gravity and dignity…in two or three words,…soberness and sense."[6] *Practicality*, however, does not necessarily mean efficiency as practiced by the secular American culture of the early twenty-first century, and the Roman Rite's concern for *simplicity* does not justify ignoring liturgical principles that are based on solid symbolic values. Too often, *liturgical* decisions nowadays are based on nonliturgical reasons in the name of so-called "simplicity and practicality," with the end result being a poor liturgy.

A simple example of misguided practicality would be the decision as to where the presiding priest stands at various points of the liturgy. The Roman Missal directs three possible places at SPECIFIC TIMES—the chair for the Introductory and Concluding Rites[7] AND ALSO FOR THE LITURGY OF THE WORD (the presiding priest needs to go to the ambo only if there is no deacon or assisting priest to read the Gospel),[8] and the altar for the Liturgy of the Eucharist. Yet how often does one see the presiding priest at the altar or the ambo for the Introductory Rites, merely because it is somewhat inconvenient to have an additional microphone at the chair. This would be an example where someone has, in the name of "simplicity and practicality," adapted the liturgy in a nonliturgical fashion.

As another example, take decisions made as to the form and shape of the eucharistic bread. Certainly the typical form and shape of the Communion breads or "hosts" as commonly found in most parishes are simple and practical, but in this case the simplicity and practicality is derived from a sense of efficiency that is alien to a fundamental symbol for the Eucharist—the symbol found in Scripture itself—the symbol of breaking one bread (cf. Luke 24, Acts 2, 1 Cor 10) from which all partake. Once again, liturgical judgments have been made based on nonliturgical concerns, much to the detriment of our worship experience.

Do not thematize what is fundamentally themeless.

We do need to focus our energies and not let our liturgies float off to never-never land. But "focusing" frequently degenerates into "what is the theme of this liturgy?" The liturgy, ANY liturgy, has only one "theme"—giving thanks to God for his action in our world as particularly expressed through Christ's death and resurrection. Anything more is frosting on the cake. When we baptize, we incorporate someone into the body of Christ and therefore into Christ's death and resurrection. When we forgive, we do so by reason of the reconciliation won by Christ's death and resurrection. And so on with the rest of the liturgical rites.

Frequently, however, planning groups struggle so much to find the "theme" and to make everything match, that damage is done to the liturgical experience.

Father Hovda wrote:

Properly understood, the theme is a modest attempt to capture in a few sentences a message in the readings in the context both of the year and of the local human situation. However, the theme gets out of hand more frequently than one would wish....Blessing God with thanks and praise is the fundamental and sufficient theme for any liturgical celebration.[9]

Benedictine Father Patrick Regan comments as follows:

Preoccupation with theme is as foreign to liturgy as it is to celebration in general. Celebration stems from

events, not abstract concepts. Of course, thematic services do make use of evangelical events, but only insofar
as they bear upon the chosen theme. By subordinating
the gospel event to a previously agreed upon theme, the
participants do not surrender to the event on its own
terms, but grasp only that aspect of it which pertains to
their purpose, thereby closing themselves to the possibility of receiving the event as it reveals and confers
itself in its own freedom, and receiving instead more
confirmation of their own thematic construct. This is
neither celebration nor liturgy. It is self-gratification.[10]

Often a theme is provided by the feast or strong season
being celebrated at the liturgy. For example, Christmas is about
the birth of our Savior—that is theme enough—one need not
examine the (four different sets of) readings to find another
theme. Similarly, Lent provides us with a time of preparation for
recelebrating the Paschal events of the death and resurrection
of Christ and a time to prepare catechumens for their baptism.
In this general context, the various Sundays of Lent offer specific ways in which our thoughts can be renewed as we attempt
to re-create our lives in Christ by remembering the sacred
moments of his death and resurrection.

In this way, "theme" provides the ambience, the atmos-
phere (like a good restaurant) for "enjoying" the (sacred) meal.
But it does not so dominate the celebration as to put the assembly, the presiding priest, and the Spirit of God into a liturgical
straightjacket from which they cannot break forward into
greater freedom before each other, and before God our Father.

I suggest that many liturgies would be improved if people
thought not so much in terms of "themes," which are usually
passive and abstract, but rather in terms of "thrusts,"
"events," "challenges"—concepts that are more active and
concrete.

Never turn the exceptional into the ordinary.

Liturgical practices should be based on an ideal, not a minimal. Certainly it is licit to administer baptism by pouring only a few drops of water over a child's forehead, but liturgical practice should be based on something which is symbolically more authentic, and the ideal for baptism is immersion (even if it cannot be done in every instance)![11] Similarly, it may be tolerated to have Communion under one kind in large gatherings (e.g., a few thousand people), but arguing for Communion under one kind in a small group simply to save a few minutes does not seem to be in the spirit of the revised liturgy.[12]

When adapting the liturgy, do not regularly omit certain options.

Making use of various options is basically the same sage advice found in the Directory for Masses with Children (#40, DOL-2173). It suggests that, for example, the Introductory Rites should be adapted for Masses with children, but that the various items that are omitted should be rotated, so that no one item is always omitted. This is wise advice for all liturgies, adapted or not. Some parishes and priests never use the option of blessing water for sprinkling in lieu of the act of penitence, for example. Some priest presiders always use option 1 or option 3 for the act of penitence. Some always omit the washing of hands. These may not be wise moves, both for continuity with the universal Church and for a varied liturgy.

Avoid the "fireman" approach to liturgy.

In the pre-Vatican II era, it was a very common practice to have all the clergy at a parish on "fireman" duty all Sunday morning. One priest said Mass and, at the right moment, another cleric would rush into the sanctuary to give the sermon. When that was done, the preacher left for another cup of coffee (unless he had to say a later Mass) only to return (with the rest of the parish "troops") to distribute Communion and then magically disappear again. Like firemen at a fire, they appeared from nowhere when needed, and then disappeared when the "emergency" was over.

The present Roman Missal is based on a renewed spirit of liturgical authenticity. Priests should not dress like deacons, ever.[13] Super-monsignors should not dress like bishops.[14] Bread should look like food.[15] Communion should be distributed under both kinds when possible.[16] In our contemporary liturgical ambience, to have someone who is *not* a part of the total liturgical experience (i.e., not present *throughout* the liturgy) exercise a significant liturgical ministry (e.g., homilist or minister of Communion) is compromising the authenticity of the symbol, and therefore leading to a poorer overall liturgy.[17]

Certainly there are circumstances that arise and even regularly exist in which the "fireman" approach must be tolerated. But, while tolerating this less-than-ideal situation, those in charge should attempt to consider alternatives that would virtually eliminate the various practices (e.g., presiding priests homilizing, increasing the number of extraordinary Communion ministers).

Do not ignore the presidential chair.

The presidential chair is a focal point of the liturgical action. It (and the ambo) are used even in those rites when the Eucharist is not celebrated, for example the Liturgy of the Hours. It is symbolic of the need we have in human societies of someone to "chair" the meeting, or of the custom in many families of referring to "daddy's special chair." The 2002 GIRM prescribes the use of the chair even when a priest celebrates Mass with only one minister present.[18] Liturgically, the presidential chair plays the same role in the typical church as the *cathedra* or bishop's chair plays in the diocesan cathedral—it is symbolic of leadership for the community. It is NOT MERELY A CONCESSION TO HUMAN WEAKNESS, but rather a symbol.[19] In most Byzantine parish churches, a special chair is reserved for the bishop, even though he might use it only once every few years. Father Hovda reminds us that the chair is *not disposable*.[20] Nevertheless, it is a place that should help the presiding priest preside over the assembly both with strength and with concern, and, thus, the chair should not be a throne.

When concelebrants are present, they should realize that presiding is a function of one person, not a committee, and there must be only ONE PRESIDENTIAL CHAIR. The sanctuary should not be rearranged so that it looks as if the board of trustees of a school are jointly presiding over a graduation, or the board of directors of a corporation are jointly presiding over a meeting of stockholders. Concelebrants should be discreetly seated on the side—for they are more a part of the assembly than appendages to the principal celebrant.[21]

The late Father Eugene Walsh, ss, offers these thoughts:

> The principle that determines, before all else, the best place for the presiding celebrant is what provides his immediate 'presence' to the celebrating community....Nothing should interfere with the immediacy of his contact with the community....The presiding celebrant does not need a throne...[but he] should have an attractive chair....[F]or the strongest sign of leadership, the presiding celebrant should be seated alone.[22]

Never put a small cross on the altar.

The Tridentine Missal prescribed that the presiding priest had to look at the corpus on the altar cross at specific times (e.g., during the "offertory prayers"). This is no longer required and, in fact, the current missal specifically requires that the major cross be "clearly visible" to the assembly (GIRM #308). Major signs are not duplicated in the new liturgy (GIRM #318); hence, there should not be a second cross on the altar solely for the benefit of the presiding priest.

Never omit silence.

Most priest presiders do include a period of silence after Communion, before the prayer after Communion, but often this silence is broken by the purification of the sacred vessels. True silence is a silence for the entire assembly only when *everyone* is silently praying and no one, not even the one presiding, is doing anything. Moreover, only relatively few presiders take advantage of other places for silence, for example, after the invitation, "Let us pray," before the collect, after each of the readings, after the homily. These should also be true moments of silence, and not merely cursory nods in that direction.[23]

Give proper, but not exaggerated, reverence to the tabernacle.

If the Blessed Sacrament is reserved somewhere in the sanctuary, a genuflection is to be made toward the tabernacle when the ministers arrive at the sanctuary or leave it at the end of Mass, but *not* during Mass itself (GIRM #274). The general principle is that one should not over-reverence the reserved

Sacrament during a ceremony whose culmination is the Sacrament that is reserved![24]

In fact, #49 of the *Ceremonial of Bishops* (CB) prescribes that if a bishop celebrates at an altar at which the Sacrament is normally reserved in a tabernacle, the Sacrament is to be *removed* during the liturgy; and the missal reiterates the principle that the tabernacle should not be on the altar at which Mass is celebrated (GIRM #315). Also, if the tabernacle is in a separate Blessed Sacrament chapel, one does not genuflect toward it when passing in procession (CB #71, GIRM #274).

Caution should be used not to reintroduce pre-Vatican II practices into the post-Vatican II liturgy.

The proverb "Actions speak louder than words" also applies in liturgical matters and it seems many priests learn more from watching other priests preside at Mass than from reading the rubrics in the missal. The current GIRM and Order of Mass eliminated a number of pre-Vatican II practices such as blessing the water before pouring it into the wine, elaborate incensation practices during the preparation of the gifts, holding the host over the chalice at the doxology, making a sign of the cross with a particle of the host before the commingling, making a sign of the cross with the host before receiving Communion. Yet it is not unusual to see such now-eliminated practices still being included at Mass.[25] Priests who notice other priests doing something "differently" might do well to check the GIRM and the rubrics in the Order of Mass before introducing any such practices themselves.

NOTES

1. *Constitution on the Liturgy* #10, DOL-10.

2. *Constitution on the Liturgy* #9, DOL-9.

3. Cf. Hovda, *Strong, Loving and Wise,* p. 30.

4. Ibid.

5. *Music in Catholic Worship* ##42–49.

6. Cf. Bishop, "The Genius of the Roman Rite," in *Liturgica Historica,* London and Toronto: OUP, 1918, 1962, pp. 12, 19. Quoted in the Canadian *Bulletin,* v. 11, #62 (Jan.–Feb. 1978), p. 46; v. 17, #95 (Sept.–Oct. 1984), p. 196, note 2.

7. Cf. GIRM ##124, 183.

8. Cf. GIRM ##136, 138.

9. Hovda, *Strong, Loving and Wise,* p. 28.

10. Regan, "Liturgy and the Experience of Celebration," *Worship* (Dec. 1973), p. 600.

11. Christian Initiation: General Introduction, n. 22.

12. Cf. GIRM ##85, 282.

13. Cf. GIRM #114; also see the Introduction to the 1972 changes in the GIRM, DOL-1372.

14. Cf. *Pontificalia Insignia,* #6, DOL-4454.

15. GIRM #321.

16. GIRM ##85, 281–282; Norms for the Celebration and Reception of Holy Communion Under Both Kinds in the Dioceses of the United States of America, #17–21.

17. Cf. GIRM #206 regarding the prohibition against priests joining a Mass as concelebrants once the liturgy has begun.

18. Cf. GIRM #256.

19. Cf. Emminghaus, *The Eucharist,* pp. 111–112.

20. Cf. Hovda, *Strong, Loving and Wise,* p. 54.

21. Cf. *Environment and Art* #70. Also see 1999 U.S. Guidelines for the Concelebration of the Eucharist, #12.

22. Walsh, *Practical Suggestions for Celebrating Sunday Mass,* pp. 18–19.

23. Cf. GIRM ##45, 56.

24. There are some significant clarifications in the revision of 1975 GIRM #233 regarding genuflections. In the corresponding expanded number of 2002 GIRM, #274, the former clause "whenever anyone passes in front of the Blessed Sacrament" has been deleted and clarified by new text. The revised text now states that genuflections before the tabernacle do *not* occur "during the celebration of Mass itself," but that "otherwise" all should genuflect, "unless they are moving in procession," in accordance with the norms in CB #71.

25. One should note that the general prohibition against adding, removing, or changing anything in the Mass (*Constitution on the Sacred Liturgy* #22; GIRM #24) also applies to reintroducing liturgical practices now omitted.

THE INTRODUCTORY RITES

Do not bow to the cross instead of the altar.

The Tridentine Missal prescribed a bow to the altar before the presiding priest opened the missal and then started the prayers at the foot of the altar. This rubric, however, was worded in a very interesting way. It mentioned the profound bow to the "altar," that is, "the image of the Crucified One placed above it" (*et Altari, seu imagini Crucifixi desuper positæ, profunde se inclinat*).[1] This suggests that the reverence was primarily to the cross and NOT to the altar. The present missal (GIRM #122, 275b) simply prescribes a bow to the altar *without* any mention of the altar cross. Since the altar cross may actually be the processional cross, it would be very awkward for the presiding priest and other ministers to have to orient themselves toward the one holding the cross to bow toward it. (Note that if one genuflects toward the Blessed Sacrament, one should not omit the bow toward the altar!)

Beware that various ministers also "misorient" themselves during prayer at other times, for example, bowing, before the Gospel, toward the cross or the tabernacle instead of toward the altar (see section 6 below).

Avoid reciting the "introit."

The Foreword to the 1975 U.S. edition of the Sacramentary included this suggestion:

Since these [Introit] antiphons are too abrupt for communal recitation, it is preferable when there is no singing that the priest (or the deacon, other minister, or commentator) adapt the antiphon and incorporate it in the presentation of the Mass of the day....The adaptation of the text of the entrance antiphon for this purpose is suggested by the Congregation for Divine Worship.

This suggestion has also been included in the 2002 version of the GIRM: "48....otherwise, [the antiphon in the missal] is recited by the priest himself, who may even adapt it as an introductory explanation."

The implications of these statements are clear—the presiding priest should not ask the congregation to "join me in reciting the introit on page 42 of your missalette." It is also LESS THAN IDEAL for the priest merely to recite it himself. It is much better to use the scriptural phrase, patristic text, or ancient liturgical refrain given in the missal as the "Entrance Antiphon" as a springboard to introduce the feast or celebration and lead into the act of penitence.

Do not omit the sign of the cross.

The sign of the cross is word and gesture, and thus bears the qualities of a minor sacrament or "sacramental." It is body-worship in addition to being mind-worship. It recalls the significant gestures made in other sacramental rites—baptism, penance, confirmation, anointing, blessings. Even when some other liturgical activity takes the place of the act of penitence (such as the blessing and procession with palms), the sign of the cross should still precede the initial greeting. To omit this action is to deprive the assembly of bodily worship, and also to deprive them of the possibility of recalling with St. Paul that, as

Christians, "it behooves us to glory in the cross of our Lord Jesus Christ" (Gal 6:14).

When making the sign of the cross, do not say "Amen."

Most of us have been at a Mass in which the priest presiding began the liturgy with a strange gesture, as if he were chasing flies away from his face and trying to catch one in front of his chest, and an even stranger statement (usually spoken in one breath), something like: "In t'nay mov t'fath'r, so, nan holy spir ta men t'lord be wi tyu." Avoid duplicating this at all costs!

The "Amen" is the response of the people and NOT of the one presiding and, in the Judeo-Christian liturgical tradition, this word in particular is a unique way of allowing individuals to affirm statements made by others. Hence, the importance of the "Amen" in worship services among African-American Baptists, especially during sermons. By usurping this response, or making the sign of the cross in such a way that the assembly is unable to respond properly, the entire worship-dialogue between the one presiding and the assembly is off to a bad start. The assembly has been told (non-verbally) that the presiding priest does not want them to become involved—that he can do it all by himself. This may be the farthest thing from a given presider's mind when he absentmindedly says "Amen" to the sign of the cross, but it sets up a psychological environment that is not well suited to good worship.

Do not vary the initial greeting to lose its biblical origin.

The three sample greetings in the Roman Missal all have biblical origins. Other greetings, however, may be used in lieu of these greetings, as a comparison with other liturgical rites issued after the original 1970 missal indicates[2] and as an examination of texts used for papal liturgies indicates (usually a special "greeting" is printed, along with the other prayer texts).[3] In these cases, however, care has been taken to model the new greeting on those found in Scripture.

Do not replace the "sacred greeting" with a "secular greeting."

The late American liturgist Ralph Keifer made the following comments about the initial greeting:

> Distortion of the formal greeting ("Good morning," "The Lord is with you") is inappropriate—a violation of the ritual bond already established by the song and procession. To say something like "Good morning" is to say loud and clear that the ritual is a barrier to communication. It is felt as a break from pattern and is experienced as the celebrant's peeping over or around a wall of ritual at the people….To say either "Good morning" or to change the greeting formula into a flat statement is to treat the congregation as if they were bored or ignorant.[4]

Benedictine Father Aidan Kavanagh essentially says the same thing:

> The reason for which some presidents choose to greet the assembly with "Good morning, everybody" instead of "The Lord be with you" is difficult to fathom. It cannot be that the former is more appropriate to the assembly's purpose than the latter. Nor can it be that the first is theologically more sophisticated than the second. And since one would prefer not to entertain the possibility

that the secular greeting is a mark of clerical condescension to the simple and untutored laity, the only alternative is to attribute the secular greeting's use to presidential thoughtlessness of a fairly low order.[5]

These are both somewhat strong positions, perhaps too strong for each and every situation, but they make the point that some seemingly insignificant adaptations are not all that insignificant, if one takes a wider picture into view. Monsignor Joseph Champlin, another well-known American liturgist, takes a slightly milder approach, however.[6] He suggests that the presider might offer a simple "good morning" to the assembly in addition to the formal biblical greeting. He does grant that this somewhat duplicates the ritual greeting, and other liturgists suggest that the Introductory Rites already contain four or five beginnings. Thus, an additional greeting does not seem to be in the interests of better liturgy.

Do not turn a brief introduction into a major homily.

The Order of Mass permits the presiding priest (or deacon or another minister) to give a brief introduction after the initial greeting and before the act of penitence. Two things are important to note: (1) this introduction should come *after* the initial greeting and NOT before the sign of the cross, and (2) the introduction should be *brief.* Such an introduction, coming right after the formal liturgical greeting, is a moment to help those assembled become more fully the unified body of Christ, gathered in the Spirit, to worship God the Father. It can provide an appropriate opportunity to recall the feast of the day, but this is NOT the time to give a detailed history of the saint's life and death, nor a time for exegesis of the readings to follow.

When using the third form of the act of penitence, (1) do not speak to the Father, the Spirit, or anyone other than Christ, and (2) do not dwell on human failures, but rather proclaim Christ's mercy and saving qualities.

Many older commentaries on the Tridentine Missal incorrectly stated that the triple *Kyrie-Christe-Kyrie* was addressed to each person of the Trinity and, in fact, the medieval tropes which embellished the sung *Kyries* in fact did include invocations to the Father and the Spirit. Contemporary studies, however, have shown that this text, borrowed from Eastern liturgies, was always intended to be addressed to Christ, and Christ alone. In earliest texts, *Kyrie* (= Lord) is associated with the hymn in Philippians 2, where it is proclaimed that "Jesus Christ is LORD to the glory of God the Father." Thus, in the official examples for options for the third form of the act of penitence given in the missal, it is always Christ who is addressed, never the Father or the Spirit (or Mary, or one of the Saints).[7]

In addition, the format of this version of the act of penitence should concentrate on divine mercy rather than human faults. In practice, this means that the "invocations" should NEVER INCLUDE THE WORD "WE" (thereby focusing on human activity) although they might occasionally tolerate the word "US" or "OUR." For example, it is INCORRECT to say:

> Lord, for the times we have ignored our sisters and brothers, and looked at our own needs: Lord, have mercy.

Invocations of this style stress human failures to an undue degree for this part of the liturgy. That emphasis would be more appropriate for a litany of penitence during a Communal

Penance Service, but not as a typical proclamation of praise of God's mercy.

Rather, the sample texts in the missal always focus on Christ (and thus on the divine initiative), and any newly composed invocations for this form of the act of penitence should do likewise. For example,

> Lord Jesus, Son of God: Lord, have mercy.
> Christ Jesus, Son of Mary: Christ, have mercy.
> Lord Jesus, Word made flesh: Lord, have mercy.
>
> Lord Jesus, you are the Way: Lord, have mercy.
> Christ Jesus, you are the Truth: Christ have mercy.
> Lord Jesus, you are our Life: Lord, have mercy.
>
> You nourish our hungers: Lord, have mercy.
> You heal our infirmities: Christ, have mercy.
> You forgive our sins: Lord, have mercy.

Do not introduce a sign of the cross at the end of the act of penitence.

In the Tridentine Missal, the *Confiteor* ended with two declaratory formulae: "May almighty God have mercy on you...," followed by "May the almighty and merciful Lord grant us pardon, absolution, and remission of all our sins." It was this *second,* quasi-absolution formula that was accompanied by a sign of the cross. In the present Roman Missal, however, this second formula has been omitted and the sign of the cross has *not* been transferred to the other formula.

Reintroducing a sign of the cross into the act of penitence is ill-advised as well as being contrary to the rubrics. Such a practice tends to heighten the significance of the act of penitence, making it even more quasi-sacramental. Most liturgists, however, would prefer to downplay an independent act of penitence (and suggest omitting it whenever possible). The more authentic liturgical tradition is that minor sins are forgiven by openheartedly hearing the Word of God and partaking in the eucharistic banquet.[8] Emphasizing the act of penitence is like emphasizing hors d'oeuvres while overlooking that the primary nourishment (in this case, reconciliation) comes later.

Never modify the prayer endings so that the assembly will not be able to respond with their "Amen."

It seems such a minor adaptation to change "for ever and ever" to "for ever" or "forevermore," or to change "through Christ our Lord" to "through Jesus our Lord and brother." And, in fact, these truly are relatively minor adaptations. Yet, in terms of ritual action, of stimulus and response, of expectations, and of repetitions, such minor changes can throw an assembly off-balance and leave them hanging in midair. If the assembly does not know when to say its proper response because the priest presiding has changed the cues, in effect the leader of prayer has deprived the assembly of its rightful part in the liturgical action! Relative to the number of words that the presiding priest says in course of the liturgy, the assembly's parts are minimal. So it is extremely important that all in the assembly be able and encouraged to say everything that is rightfully theirs. The few "Amen's" of the liturgy may seem insignificant, but they are extremely important in meaning, for they allow the local assembly, the microcosmic incarnation of the Christian Church, to affirm (since "Amen" = "I agree" = "Yes, it is true") what the leader of prayer has just finished praying, and thus make that prayer their own.

The collect (or "opening prayer") concludes the entrance procession and introductory rites—it does not (of its nature) introduce the readings.

In the Roman liturgical tradition, on Sundays and major feasts the same prayer is used to conclude the Office of Readings, Morning Prayer, and Evening Prayer from the Liturgy of the Hours, and as the collect at Mass. In the tradition, this prayer expresses general sentiments appropriate for any communal worship service. It can and does refer to any feast of the church being celebrated that day, and in that sense often appropriately prepares the assembly to hear the word of God. Of its nature, however, it need not directly refer to the readings that follow and should serve more as a summation of the sentiments of the assembly, gathered in prayer, attentive to God's presence, and mindful of their needs and deficiencies. The missals of Holland and Italy include optional collects for Sundays in Ordinary Time that do blend more with the readings assigned for those days, and other Christian denominations, such as the Presbyterian Church in the U.S.A., have produced similar collections of prayers for their eucharistic liturgies. In every instance, however, such prayers still serve as general gathering prayers, whose language is inspired by the readings that follow, but not as prayers that introduce the readings per se.

Beware of unofficial prayers.

The following is a quotation from a well-known bishop, writing about some of the prayers he found his priests using:

The prayers of many are being corrected every day, once they have been read by the learned, and much against catholic faith is found in them. Many blindly seize upon prayers composed not only by unskilled babblers but even by heretics and use them because in their simple ignorance they cannot evaluate the prayers and think them good.

The bishop was St. Augustine (354–430), and he was referring to prayers used to bless baptismal water.[9] But the same sentiments can be expressed concerning prayers one hears today, particularly in informal and small group liturgies. The prayers in the missal are not perfect, but at least no one's faith will be led astray by them. That is not necessarily true with prayers found elsewhere, or those composed by members of a local liturgy committee, or those which the presiding priest prays extemporaneously.

NOTES

1. *Ritus servandus in Celebratione Missæ:* II—*De Ingressu Sacerdotis ad Altare,* sec. 2.

2. E.g., Rite for Distributing Communion Outside of Mass, #27.

3. Cf. *Notitiæ,* the semi-official journal of the Congregation for the Sacraments and Divine Worship, which reprints many of the newly composed texts for papal liturgies (e.g., *Notitiæ,* v. 12, n. 1 [Jan. 1976], p. 17, *Missa Votiva «Pro Pace»*).

4. Keifer, *To Give Thanks and Praise,* p. 109.

5. Kavanagh, *Elements of Rite,* p. 77.

6. Champlin, *The Proper Balance,* pp. 81–82.

7. Cf. Bishops' Committee on the Liturgy [BCL], *Newsletter,* v. 10, ##6-7 (June–July 1974), pp. 428–29. Note that the Polish Missal explicitly labels the third form of the act of penitence as "Invocations to Christ."

8. *CCC* ##1434–39.

9. Augustine, *De bapt. contra Donastistas,* 6.47; quoted in Allan Bouley, O.S.B., *From Freedom to Formula,* p. 165.

THE LITURGY OF THE WORD

Use only one ambo for proclaiming all and only the word of God.

Contemporary liturgical writers emphasize the importance of ONE ambo from which ALL and ONLY the word of God is proclaimed and nothing else. If another book stand is used (by musicians or commentators or even the one presiding), it should be significantly different. This is not merely the preference of liturgists—it is found in nearly all major documents and contemporary liturgical writers.

For example, in the missal, we find the norms:

GIRM #58: In the celebration of the Mass with a congregation, the readings are always proclaimed from the ambo.

GIRM #309: The dignity of the ambo requires that only a minister of the word should go up to it.

as well as the caution:

GIRM #105b: ...the commentator stands in an appropriate place facing the faithful, but not at the ambo.

The *Introduction to the Lectionary* presents these additional comments for our consideration:

32. There must be a place [for proclaiming the word of God] in the church that is somewhat elevated, fixed, and of suitable design and nobility. It should reflect the dignity of God's word and be a clear reminder to the people that in the Mass the table of God's word and of Christ's body is placed before them.

33. Either permanently or at least on occasions of greater solemnity, the ambo should be decorated.

34. In order that the ambo may properly serve its liturgical purpose, it is to be rather large, since on occasion several ministers must use it at the same time.

In *Environment and Art* we read:

A very simple lectern, in no way competing or conflicting with the main ambo…can be used by a cantor, song leader, commentator, and reader of the announcements.[1]

and *Built of Living Stones* tells us:

61. The central focus of the area in which the word of God is proclaimed during the liturgy is the *ambo*. The design of the ambo and its prominent placement reflects the dignity and nobility of that saving word and draws the attention of those present to the proclamation of the word.*

Intro. Lect., #32 (text above). Cf. GIRM #309 (excerpt on previous page).

89. Apart from the singing of the Responsorial Psalm, which normally occurs at the ambo, the stand for the cantor or song leader is distinct from the ambo, which is reserved for the proclamation of the word of God.

The 1970 U.S. Appendix to General Instruction of the Roman Missal expanded on the general norm by noting:

> The reservation of a single place for all the biblical readings is more significant than the person of the reader, whether ordained or lay, whether woman or man.[2]

In 1980, the late Dr. Ralph Keifer wrote the following to help explain the general norm found in the missal (note that he used "lectern" where today we would use "ambo"):

> The Sacramentary indicates a preference for using a single lectern. On special occasions (especially for the reading of the Passion), special arrangements can be made. Proclaiming the Word from one place (most of the time) makes the Word prominent in the arrangement of the worship space, a space which communicates a sense of priorities in worship. The Word will lose its prominence if the lectern is the same size as the music stand, or if the sanctuary says in its arrangement that the Word is unimportant and can be proclaimed any old place, or even if the lectern looks like an appendage to the altar. It is just as appropriate and just as desirable to place candles or flowers near the lectern as it is to place them near the altar....Just as the Lectionary should not be a repository for notes, as the chalice and paten are not used as cruet holders, neither is the lectern the place for making announcements or leading music. The lectern should be reverenced by using it for its holy purpose—proclaiming the Word—just as the altar is reverenced by not using it as a lavabo towel rack or a stand for a portable font.[3]

In some churches one may still find two reading stands set up on either side of the altar, with the presiding priest using one of the stands or the altar for his part of the Mass, while the lay lector uses the other. In contrast to such a practice, the missal directs that only the Liturgy of the Word should take place at the ambo (GIRM #309) and only the Liturgy of the Eucharist at the altar—the presiding priest should remain at the chair for the Introductory and Concluding Rites (also see section 4). If a different "choreography" is being followed, it is usually because the liturgical judgment is being made based on something else—where microphones are available rather than whether something is good liturgy. In using separate reading stands for priest and laity, we are also symbolically saying that it is more important to keep clergy and laity separate than to show forth the unity of God's word.

Never proclaim God's word from disposable missalettes or typewritten pages.

In the *Introduction to the Lectionary* we read:

37. Because of the dignity of the word of God, the books of readings used in the celebration are not to be replaced by other pastoral aids, for example, by leaflets printed for the preparation of the readings by the faithful or for their personal meditation.

Frequently pastors and people are caught in a mutual bind—lectors are so poor that no one in the assembly can truly understand the proclamation of God's word, so the church must be filled with missalettes. But that is no excuse for the use of missalettes by the ministers of the word. To read God's "two-edged sword" from a disposable missalette is like putting the Blood of the Lord into paper cups—most Catholics would be aghast at the latter, but do not bat an eye at the former. Yet in the realm of symbol, both are equivalent. The word of God is present in the Bread and Wine of the Eucharist and the containers we use for the Sacred Bread and Precious Wine should mirror our faith in Christ's presence. But the word of God is also present in the Scriptures proclaimed and we attest to that presence by using physical books indicative of our belief in the importance of God's written word in our lives. Nothing less will do.

One might also reflect on why we are not more sensitive to reading God's word from an appropriate book. Once again, this may be a situation of *ex opere operato* still reigning supreme. Since the words spoken are the same, whether they are printed in a magnificent, well-bound Book of the Gospels, or a newspaper print missalette, the "how" aspect is overlooked. In addition, the Catholic bias to seeing the only "real" presence of Christ as that which is in the Eucharist causes our sensibilities to demand well-made and artistic chalices and patens encrusted with jewels, but at the same time to ignore the equally "real" presence of Christ in Scripture! (I do grant, however, that the scriptural real presence is of a theologically different category than the eucharistic real presence, but both are still *real*.)

Never handle the lectionary as if it were a novel.

Especially in smaller liturgies, there is a temptation to put the book of readings away, after its use, in some "convenient" location where it is "out of the way," and this often means on the floor or under a chair. Once again, an equivalent action would be to put a ciborium still filled with consecrated hosts under a chair or on the floor. We would shudder at the latter, but we frequently see nothing wrong with the former. It is part of the Byzantine tradition that the Book of the Gospels always remains on the altar until it is used for the actual proclamation. Many ambos are being constructed with a "throne" for the lectionary or Book of the Gospels, so that immediately after use it may be placed where it can be reverenced for what it contains—God's holy word.[4] Yet, how often does one see a homilist put his notes on top of God's word—or take the holy words and put them in an insignificant place, so that his human words can take their place? This might be considered by some as being tantamount to arrogance (if we look at it on the symbolic level). This seemingly minor action should not be overlooked either, since it deals with basic symbols of the liturgy—God's presence in Scripture and how we physically handle the visible Scriptures. Liturgy is basically about helping each other find God's presence in the symbols that surround us, a long and oftentimes tedious process! Thus we should not downplay one of the more obvious liturgical symbols of that divine presence.

Never hide the book of God's written word.

The books of God's written word are the "chalices" of that word, and should be handled as such. Just as the chalice and paten are held high at the end of the eucharistic prayer, so the lectionary and the Book of the Gospels should be held so that the congregation sees them and accepts them as the symbols for what they contain—God's nourishment for a holy people. In particular, it is appropriate to carry the Book of the Gospels elevated in procession to the altar during the entrance and from the altar to the ambo during the *Alleluia* or Lenten substitute (cf. GIRM #133, 175), and it is better to hold the lectionary and Book of the Gospels when reading from them at the ambo so that they may be seen by the assembly, rather than leaving them semi-hidden on the ambo. A book of Scripture may rest on the ambo when not actively being used, but when it is actually used for the proclamation it should be visible as the sacrament of God's presence.

As a fitting conclusion to the reading, the lector should pause in silence (cf. GIRM #45, *Intro. Lect.* #28) and then announce, "The word [Gospel] of the Lord!" Although it is permitted for a bishop, if he is presiding at Mass, to bless the assembly with the Book of the Gospels after the proclamation of the Gospel (GIRM #175), it may be better not to draw attention to the books of Scripture after the proclamation of a reading (for example, by lifting the book high), but to focus instead on the word heard by those present and received into their hearts.

Priests should not read the non-gospel readings if others who can read are available.

Both the missal (GIRM #99) and the lectionary (*Intro. Lect.* #51) reiterate a liturgical tradition concerning the ministry of reading Scripture in the liturgical assembly. It is a proper function which differs from the office of leadership belonging to deacon and priest. Therefore, even if there are many deacons and priests available, the reading of Scripture (except for the Gospel) should be done by non-ordained lectors.

The response to the first reading must be a psalm (or its liturgical equivalent).

We are frequently put into a no-win situation: the response to the first reading should be sung—but one does not easily obtain singable psalm texts. Therefore, there is a tendency to choose an "appropriate" song as a substitute. Sometimes, these appropriate songs are even based on Scripture, but are not from the psalter. This practice, besides being contrary to liturgical norms, is less than ideal and should be avoided.

It is permitted to use an alternative psalm in lieu of the psalm given in the lectionary for a given day, but the alternative must be from the psalter (or its liturgical equivalent, e.g., the Magnificat, the Benedictus, or some other Old Testament canticle, as the Song of Hannah). In the context of the structure of the Liturgy of the Word, we (i.e., the assembly) use God's word to respond to God's word. Thus the texts should be from Scripture.

And our response should be a true *response*. The psalms were meant to be sung by an assembly in praise of the God of Israel. The wording is such that the psalm addresses God directly (Ps 51—Have mercy on me, O God), or is an exhortation to the self (Ps 104—Bless the Lord, O my soul) or to others to praise God (Ps 95—Come, let us worship the Lord). Using other sections of Scripture may seem to fit in with the "theme," but, as a way of enabling the assembly to give voice to the Lord, they are problematic since, at times, some of these songs quote God addressing his people. This results in a somewhat odd situation in which the assembly is using God's exhortation to them and addressing that exhortation back to God.

Those who preside should make sure that other ministers perform their ministry well. In particular, make sure that lectors always help the assembly with the psalm response.

An amazing number of lectors never help the assembly respond to the psalm, by repeating the psalm response audibly. It is as if these lectors are oblivious to the fact that the majority of the assembly does not have the text of the response in front of them. The one who proclaims the psalm should both proclaim the verses in such a way that the assembly knows when to answer (normally dropping the tone of his or her voice at the end of each verse), and help those present by proclaiming the response vigorously whenever the assembly is supposed to proclaim it. Most responses are not that difficult to remember, but they are not totally memorized after merely one try.

Never recite the *Alleluia!*

In the missal, GIRM #63c states: "The *Alleluia* or the verse before the Gospel may be omitted if they are not sung." But practice has shown that not omitting the *Alleluia* leads to insipid "Acclamations of Joy!" which are neither acclamatory nor joyful. *The Introduction to the Lectionary* words its norm to eliminate the option and flatly states (emphasis added),

> 23. The *Alleluia* or the verse before the Gospel *must be sung,* and during it all stand. It is not to be sung only by the cantor who intones it or by the choir, but by the whole of the people together.[5]

The presiding priest should never read the Gospel if another priest or deacon is present.

The missal gives us this principle:

> GIRM #59: By tradition, the function of proclaiming the readings is ministerial, not presidential. The readings, therefore, should be proclaimed by a lector, and the Gospel by a deacon or, in his absence, a priest other than the celebrant.

This principle is also repeated in the *Introduction to the Lectionary* (#49).

When present, a deacon seeks and receives a blessing from the presiding priest,[6] but another priest does not, unless the presider be a bishop.[7]

Some presiding priests suggest that since they will deliver the homily, they should also proclaim the Gospel because of its intimate connection. It is true that the homily should be intimately connected with the Scripture that precedes it, but this proposed rule would also suggest that the homilist should proclaim *all* the Scripture which is referred to in his homily, not merely the Gospel. Proclaiming the *message* of Scripture by giving a homily is a presidential function, but proclaiming the *text* of Scripture by reading a pericope from the lectionary or Book of the Gospels is a ministerial function. These two actions should not be confused and one way of keeping the roles separate is to insist that the presider never proclaims the Gospel if another priest or deacon is present.

Never bow to the tabernacle or the cross when reciting the preparation prayer before proclaiming the Gospel.

If no other deacon or priest is available, then the presiding priest himself proclaims the Gospel and prepares himself by reciting a prayer inspired by Isaiah 6:7. The missal (GIRM #132) prescribes that the presiding priest should bow TOWARDS THE ALTAR while reciting this prayer. Frequently, however, one sees priests bowing toward the TABERNACLE instead, as if it were "more reverential" to bow toward the reserved Sacrament. Besides being contrary to the rubrics, this action puts more emphasis on the reserved Sacrament than good liturgy suggests should be done. The reserved Sacrament should be seen as the fruit of the Eucharist—therefore, as noted in section 4, it is inconsistent to "interrupt" the liturgy to make reverence to the reserved Sacrament. During the liturgy, the altar is the primary architectural symbol of Christ (cf. GIRM #298), and must be reverenced as such.

Do not omit gesture at the Gospel.

Since the Gospel is the climax of the Liturgy of the Word, special gestures and postures have been traditionally used to enhance this special word. The assembly stands. Candles and incense may accompany the proclamation. The minister and assembly cross themselves on the forehead, lips, and heart. The minister reverences the text with a kiss at the end. In the Russian and Greek usages of the Byzantine Rite and at papal liturgies, after the Greek proclamation of the Gospel the assembly is blessed by the presiding priest with the Book of the Gospels, and such a blessing is now also permitted if a bishop presides at Mass (GIRM #175). All these gestures help the assembly focus on the specialness of the Gospel and, as mentioned above, involve the assembly in body-worship as well as mind-worship. Thus, the omission of any of these gestures should not be undertaken lightly!

It is preferred that the homily be given from the chair.

The *Introduction to the Lectionary* reiterates an ancient tradition in #26: "The priest celebrant gives the homily either at the chair, standing or sitting, or at the ambo."[8] This emphasizes a tradition that was observed by bishops but overlooked by others—that delivering a homily is part of the presidential office, and thus should be delivered at the place where the presiding priest presides—the chair. Also following an ancient episcopal tradition (CB #142), the presiding priest may sit while preaching the homily.

Do not begin or end the homily with a sign of the cross.

In the early 1970s, a question about this practice, along with whether it is appropriate to use a greeting to the assembly to begin the homily, was posed to the Congregation for Divine Worship. The answer given was:

> …generally speaking it is inadvisable to continue such customs because they have their origin in preaching outside Mass. The homily is part of the liturgy; the people have already blessed themselves and received the greeting at the beginning of Mass. It is better, then, not to have a repetition before or after the homily.[9]

Do not give a sermon, but rather "break the bread of the word" with a homily.

A sermon is a holy speech, a sacred oration—but, of its nature, it need not be connected to Scripture. A homily should start with the context of the celebration, particularly the feast being celebrated, or, if there is no feast, the experience of the Scripture just proclaimed. It should be a holy reflection on the Scripture, "breaking the bread" of God's written word for the assembly so that those present can be nourished by it (cf. GIRM #65). It should offer practical applications to the contemporary experience, and a challenge to the way lives are lived in the contemporary culture. It is not an academic lecture containing absolute truth as perceived by the homilist, but a humble sharing of God's graces and insights for the building up of God's priestly people. Most authors suggest that, ideally, the homily should be only around 7 to 10 minutes long on a typical Sunday, and 4 to 6 minutes long on a weekday. A special occasion might be able to tolerate a homily of 12 or 14 minutes. Homilies longer than 15 minutes, however, are usually an imposition on the psyches of members of the assembly. In addition, oftentimes, "homilists" who go longer than 15 minutes have not said anything that could not have been said in the first five minutes anyway. Some homilists have a bad habit of multiplying words so that (both they and) the assembly do not realize that there is no real substance![10]

Do not change the structure of the prayer of the faithful.

Some individuals seem to have a very difficult time understanding the basic paradigm given in the missal for the prayer of the faithful (general intercessions). The normal structure consists of four main sections: an *Introduction* by the PRESIDING PRIEST; the *Invitations of Concern* (i.e., PETITIONS) by the DEACON, CANTOR, or LECTOR; the *Response of Prayer* by the ASSEMBLY; a *Final Concluding Prayer* by the PRESIDING PRIEST.

Note some of the implications of this structure: (1) The PRIEST WHO PRESIDES *always* introduces and concludes this part of the liturgy—the introduction and conclusion should never be delegated to another priest or, worse still, to the deacon or the lector. (2) The PRESIDING PRIEST should *never* offer the invitations of concern (i.e., petitions) unless no one else who is competent is present. (3) The so-called *petitions* are *invitations* to prayer—they are statements addressed TO THE ASSEMBLY inviting them to pray for specific topics of *concern*. In themselves these *petitions* are NOT PRAYERS addressed to GOD THE FATHER or to JESUS! (This also holds true for the introduction by the presiding priest—it is NOT a prayer to God. Rather, it is a statement to the assembly, inviting them to join in prayer for the intentions that will be proposed.) The actual *prayer* is said by the assembly together and, in the United States, usually is "Lord, hear our prayer."

Let me offer one further comment about the *petitions*. What frequently happens when the petitions are reworded into mini-prayers to Christ is that we are left with a series of grammatically incorrect statements—most of each petition is addressed to the Lord and the last phrase, "let us pray to the Lord," is addressed to the assembly. The assembly is barraged with a series of schizophrenic statements. No wonder they frequently don't know how to react!

Do not change the intercessions to prayers of thanks.

Sometimes, one hears petitions that read something like, "For Mary and Joe, IN THANKSGIVING for all they mean to us, let us pray to the Lord." Although such a petition somewhat retains the general form for an intercession, it basically states a motive for thanksgiving, and thanksgiving belongs during, or before, the eucharistic prayer.

Do not over-localize the prayer of the faithful.

Especially in small groups, the petitions of the prayer of the faithful can become so localized, praying for intra-community concerns, that one can forget that the local community is part of a wider church. The prayer of the faithful provides an opportunity for the local church to reach out to the Church Universal in prayer, in concern, and (one would hope) in action.

Remember that the prayer of the faithful is basically a litany.

The prayer of the faithful forms a litany, and litanies are meant to be sung in a mantra-like style inducing an ambience of prayer. Paying more attention to the "how" of the intercessions (i.e., by singing them), than to the "what" (i.e., the text) may produce marvelous and unexpected results!

NOTES

1. *Environment and Art,* 75.

2. 1970 U.S. Appendix to the GIRM, comments on section #66 of the 1969 GIRM.

3. Keifer, *To Give Thanks and Praise,* pp. 120–121.

4. Cf. *Built of Living Stones,* #62.

5. BCL *Newsletter,* v. XXI (October 1985), p. 39.

6. GIRM #175; *Introduction to Lectionary* #17.

7. GIRM #212; *Ceremonial of Bishops* #74, 173.

8. The Latin text reads: *"homiliam profert ad sedem, stans vel sedens,"* although recent versions of the *Introduction to the Lectionary* published in the United States have omitted the reference to sitting at the chair.

9. Cf. *Notitiæ,* v. 9 (1973), p. 178, DOL–1432: note R8; *Fulfilled In Your Hearing: The Homily in the Sunday Assembly,* note 7.

10. Cf. also *Fulfilled In Your Hearing.*

THE LITURGY OF THE EUCHARIST

Do not ignore the four-fold biblical structure of the Liturgy of the Eucharist!

In the narratives of the Last Supper found in the synoptic Gospels and Paul (1 Cor 11), in the narrative of the miracles of the multiplications of the loaves and fishes, and in the post-resurrection appearances of the Lord (e.g., the Easter appearance at Emmaus), again and again we find the meals described using four verbs: TAKE, BLESS, BREAK, and GIVE. These four actions shape the Liturgy of the Eucharist in all liturgical families. Yet in the Liturgy of the Eucharist, we *do not dramatically reenact* the Last Supper scene, but rather *liturgically remember* what occurs and incorporate the verbs into the structure of our worship. This last point is more important than it looks. Since the four verbs are so prominent in Scripture, we cannot totally overlook them and still claim to be in continuity with the tradition. These four verbs *structure* our worship, but not in a way that the eucharistic liturgy becomes a dramatic reenactment of the Last Supper, as was done in the musicals *Godspell* and *Jesus Christ, Superstar.*

In the Christian liturgical tradition, TAKING has given rise to the procession with the gifts and their preparation and placement on the altar, BLESSING has given rise to the eucharistic prayer, BREAKING has been preserved in the fraction rite (the rite of the breaking of the bread), and GIVING becomes the reception of Communion (cf. GIRM #72). To telescope two of these rites together is to do damage to the structure of the liturgy (e.g., breaking the bread during the eucharistic prayer).

Similarly, not to give proper emphasis to one of these rites is also to do damage to the structure of the liturgy (e.g., downplaying or hiding the breaking of the bread).

In addition, to change the nature of the rite is, once again, to do damage to the structure of the liturgy. For example, TAKING, BREAKING, GIVING are actions, NOT words, and thus any words spoken should not overwhelm or obscure the actions taking place. Consequently, in particular, one should not turn the reception and preparation of the gifts into a series of "offering" prayers, since this would be turning what is fundamentally an action (taking) into words (prayers).

Never plan on using hosts from the tabernacle at Mass—or, correlatively—always consecrate enough bread and wine to minister to those present.

An examination of the various Vatican liturgical documents issued since the Second Vatican Council reveals an interesting fact. Nowhere is it explicitly mentioned that consecrated hosts already in the tabernacle may be used during the Communion rite at Mass!

All the documents mention the necessity of reverence before the reserved Sacrament, of how it is lawful and encouraged to pray before the tabernacle, of how it is permitted to minister Communion *outside of Mass* from the tabernacle for those unable to participate in Mass (therefore also implying that it is NOT permitted to administer Communion immediately before or after Mass), and of how it is necessary to reserve the Sacrament for the sick and the dying. Whenever referring to the reserved Sacrament, however, no mention is ever made of its use during Mass.

In fact, the opposite is true. Starting at least in 1742, there was encouragement given that the faithful should receive

Communion from the elements consecrated AT THAT MASS.[1] This exhortation was quoted by Pope Pius XII in his encyclical *Mediator Dei* in 1947,[2] repeated in the Second Vatican Council's *Constitution on the Liturgy* in 1963,[3] repeated in the Roman Instruction *Eucharisticum Mysterium* in 1967,[4] repeated in the 1969 GIRM,[5] made even stronger in the 2002 GIRM,[6] and repeated in various other decrees and liturgical documents since the Council as well! It should also be noted that this practice was actually urged by the 1570 missal as well![7]

This norm does not mean that one can never use what is in the tabernacle during the Communion rite at Mass. But it does mean that our preparation should be such that we determine (perhaps by carefully counting for several weeks) how many people normally receive Communion at a given Mass and plan accordingly (by not preparing way too few or way too many hosts or other eucharistic bread). Proper preparation will mean that what is in the tabernacle will be used solely (primarily) as a focal point for prayer and as a resource for the sick. Thus, as a general rule, there should NEVER be more than one vessel (ciborium) of hosts in a tabernacle, and ideally NOT more than about 50 hosts therein. Since, in most churches, Mass is celebrated daily, that supply for the sick could easily be renewed within 24 hours! Such a general rule may seem obvious, but a common older mindset assumed that Mass was mainly to refill the tabernacle and, thus, that the tabernacle should always be filled with hosts from which the people received Communion, even during Mass. Unfortunately for good liturgy, these practices are still in vogue in some parishes!

Do not *offer* the gifts during their *preparation*— in particular, do not lift them high in the air.

The 1969 Order of Mass significantly changed what formerly occurred between the Creed and the eucharistic prayer.

In the current Order of Mass the gifts are received, prepared, and formally placed on the altar by the priest after he briefly blesses God in thanksgiving for God's gifts. Formerly, we "offered" bread and wine to God, but now we realize that offering anything other than Christ is theologically inappropriate. The real "offering" takes place during the "anamnesis" section of the eucharistic prayer, which occurs after the institution narrative and memorial acclamation.

In addition, in 1969 there was a significant change in the gestures prescribed by the rubrics, a change that many priests still seem not to have noticed (cf. GIRM #141). The Tridentine Missal required the presiding priest to hold the paten and chalice at eye level in a gesture of "offering," while looking at the corpus on the altar cross. The present missal omits this gesture because, since the cross must be seen by the assembly but not always by the priest, it can be on the back wall of the sanctuary, behind the presiding priest! In addition, the present missal speaks about holding the gifts "slightly" above the altar. The Latin word used here is *aliquantulum,* the same word used in the Tridentine Missal to describe how high the presiding priest held the chalice up during the former "minor elevation" (i.e., the doxology of the eucharistic prayer). In many rubrical commentary books, this word was interpreted as meaning "3–4 inches"[8] or "a hand's breadth."[9]

This previous paragraph's brief examination of the revised rubrics may help shed a bit more light on the present structure and purpose of this part of the liturgy. This part of the Mass should be seen primarily as a rite of *accepting the offerings* from the people, briefly *thanking God* for them, and only then *formally placing* the bread and wine upon the altar. We are trying to retrieve the ancient simplicity of this part of the liturgy. Originally, the gifts were accepted from the people and (in one sense) received an initial "sanctification" by simple contact with the altar—the basic architectural symbol of Christ (cf. GIRM #298; cf. also Matt 23:19–20 where Christ indicates that the altar makes holy the gifts placed on it). Thus, at this point of the Mass we do NOT OFFER—that will be done during the eucharistic prayer. We also should not have the gifts on the altar already—that is counter-symbolic since they should touch the altar only *after* the prayers are said. They also should not be put on the altar by the servers, deacon, or people since it is the formal duty of the presiding priest to "place" the bread and wine upon the altar (cf. GIRM ##75, 141, 142) after he accepts them from the people or deacon.

Practically, an ideal choreography might go like this. The priest accepts the gifts of bread and wine from the people and gives the wine to the deacon or server (or the deacon could accept the wine himself). (It is probably better to have the water on the credence table and not have it brought up in procession since it is a non-biblical [yet ancient] addition to the "matter" of the Eucharist.)[10] The presiding priest continues to hold the vessel with the bread while carrying it to the altar and then quietly says the appropriate prayer while holding the vessel *slightly* over the altar. Only *after* the prayer does he let the vessel with the bread touch the altar. Meanwhile, at the credence, the deacon (or concelebrant) pours the wine *and water* into the chalice (saying the prescribed prayer) and holds it (and any additional flagon or carafe) for the presiding priest until needed. Once again, only *after* the appropriate prayer does the chalice touch the altar. If there is no deacon or concelebrant, it is possible (although somewhat awkward) for the presiding priest to prepare the chalice himself at the credence, or to hold the chalice off the altar at the side while pouring the wine and water into it.

What should be avoided is the common scenario where the offerings are placed on the altar at the center once, then lifted up by the priest at eyes' level while the prayers are said, then placed on the altar again, as if the prayers were the most important point of this section of the liturgy. In the current missal, *the preparation of the gifts is fundamentally an action,* the action of placing bread and wine on the altar, and *not* a rite of *offering* in which the prayers are primary!

To reiterate, it is better to prepare the chalice at the credence table. This should be done by the deacon or concelebrant (and not the presiding priest). In addition, the water is not blessed.

The missal (GIRM #178) notes that the deacon may prepare the chalice at the credence table *saying the accompanying prayer.* In view of the historical meaning of the gifts touching the altar—the symbol of Christ—in general, preparing the chalice away from the altar would seem to be a better practice. Note that the deacon (or concelebrant) should pour *both the wine and the water* into the chalice. The sign of the cross, blessing the water, required in the Tridentine Mass, is *omitted* in the current Order of Mass.

Do not prepare the offerings at the altar while the collection is being taken.

Preparing the bread and wine at the altar while the collection is being taken is another example of doing two things at the same time and, as noted earlier, such double activities should be avoided. The collection is part of the gathering of offerings for the celebration. Some of those offerings consist of bread and wine which will be "eucharistized" through the prayer voiced by the priest who presides. Some of those offerings might also consist of specific food offerings for the poor, especially on occasions such as Holy Thursday or Thanksgiving Day. Usually, some of the offerings consist of monetary offerings used for the basic necessities of community life, such as paying utility bills and salaries. All of these items are offerings of the community to be presented to the one who presides over the community's prayer for the benefit of the community. It is improper to accept some offerings and prepare them at the altar while the other offerings are still being gathered.

Do not make a habit of saying the "offertory" prayers aloud.

Close examination of the rubrics of this point of the liturgy reveal that the first option given in the missal is for ALL the prayers (including the two "BLESSED ARE YOU,..." prayers) to be recited *quietly (secreto)* by the presiding priest (GIRM ##141, 142). The missal then gives the option that IF there is NO SINGING, the presiding priest MAY (but is not required to) say the two "BLESSED ARE YOU,..." prayers aloud (GIRM #142). If these two prayers are recited audibly, then the assembly MAY (but again is *not* required to) respond with "Blessed be God forever."[11]

This part of the liturgy corresponds to the biblical action of TAKING—which is ACTION, NOT WORDS. Thus, it is NOT primarily a time for words. In fact, the words can be counter-productive in that they can take away from the important words that follow—the eucharistic prayer.

In addition, reciting ALL the prayers audibly, rather than just the two "Blessed are you,..." prayers, makes all the prayers seem of equal value. Therefore, members of the assembly cannot sense, from what they hear, which prayers are primary and which are secondary.

Do not clutter the altar with unneeded ciboria and chalices.

Altars can sometimes look like awards tables at bowling banquets,[12] or like vendors' tables at pottery crafts shows. The missal, however, prescribes that nothing more be present other than what is necessary at the moment (cf. GIRM #306). During the Liturgy of the Eucharist we need the strong symbol of ONE BREAD and ONE CUP. If more than one container is needed because of the quantity of bread and wine needed for the assembly, then a large enough vessel should be used to be able to contain all the bread needed, and one chalice can be augmented by one (or more) large decanters, carafes, or flagons. This is a rubric in the 1983 Italian Missal[13] and is also recommended by the 2002 U.S. Norms for Communion under Both Kinds.[14]

Do not wash your fingertips—wash your hands.

In the 1965 interim revision of the rubrics of the Mass, the phrase that suggested that all the presiding priest had to do when he "washed his hands" was merely wash the thumb and index finger of both hands, was omitted. Similarly, in the present missal, the rubric simply says that the presiding priest should wash his hands (GIRM #145).

A general canonical principle is that when some law is changed in a manner such as this, the older practice is meant to be changed. In this case, the older practice was in the spirit of Roman minimalism, but the truth of the sign and symbol is that HANDS should be washed—NOT merely FINGERTIPS. Thus, the washing of hands necessitates "finger bowls" large enough for the priest to be able to wash his hands properly, and "finger towels" that can be used to dry HANDS, and not merely fingertips!

It is not uncommon to see the washing of hands omitted, either occasionally or regularly, something not generally permitted by the rubrics except occasionally in Masses with Children. The washing of hands in the Roman Rite finds its origin as a *practical* necessity following the presiding priest's acceptance of offerings from the people, and then incensing the offerings. It is unknown in many other major liturgical families. It has, however, now taken on the added *symbolic* meaning of renewing one's baptismal purification, appropriate before offering the sacrifice of praise. Thus, if performed carefully and with meaning, this simple rite can help the assembly to appreciate the connection between the purifying waters of baptism and the celebration of the Eucharist. Therefore, its omission should not be done lightly, as if no other alternatives are possible!

One might also reflect on the ways that non-Christian religions make use of the same gesture. In some versions of the Jewish Seder service, all present are invited to wash their hands as part of the ritual preparation before partaking of the Passover meal proper. Also, at some Shinto shrines there is a place near the entrance for all, believers and visitors alike, to wash their hands as a symbol of the desire for interior cleansing before entering the holy place.

The prayer over the offerings concludes the preparation rite—it does not introduce the eucharistic prayer.

The prayer over the offerings is basically the final prayer which summarizes the second major procession of the liturgy— the procession with the offerings. It corresponds to the collect, which ultimately concludes the entrance procession, and the prayer after Communion, which concludes the Communion procession. This prayer is introduced by the "Pray, brethren,..." now interpreted as an elongated form of "Let us pray" (in fact, in the German Missal the simple "Let us pray" is given as one of three options to introduce the prayer over the offerings). This prayer should mention "offering" only insofar as the bread and wine have been received and placed on the altar for the "offering" that is the sacrifice of praise vocalized in the eucharistic prayer and ratified in the reception of Communion. To reword or amend the prayer texts in order to turn the prayer over the offerings into an independent "offering" prayer, or an independent "epiclesis" prayer invoking the Spirit, is to detract from the eucharistic prayer as the primary place in which such sentiments rightfully are expressed in the tradition of Christian eucharistic worship.

Since, as mentioned above, the "Pray, brethren,…" is now viewed as an elongated "Let us pray," the presider should NOT say "Amen" after the assembly's response, "May the Lord accept…." This practice is either a misreading of the rubrics in the present missal (which says that the *assembly* responds with "Amen" after the prayer over the offerings), or a continuation of the custom prescribed in the Tridentine Missal.

Follow the rubrics regarding each of the eucharistic prayers.

In particular, Eucharistic Prayer II should not regularly be used on Sundays (since GIRM #365b specifically mentions its use is "suitable for weekdays"), and Eucharistic Prayer IV (along with the Eucharistic Prayers for Children and for Various Needs and Occasions) should not be used with any preface other than the one included as part of the prayer (cf. GIRM #365d).

Do not interrupt the eucharistic prayer for announcements.

Not interrupting the eucharistic prayer may seem logical enough, but a preliminary problem rests with understanding what really constitutes the eucharistic prayer. The eucharistic prayer begins with the introductory dialogue of the priest ("The Lord be with you"…"Lift up your hearts") and ends with the final "Great" Amen of the assembly after the doxology ("Through him,…").[15] Unfortunately, many people still think of the eucharistic prayer as being two parts (i.e., the preface with the *Sanctus,* and then the "Canon"), and some people act as if it were four parts (i.e., preface with *Sanctus;* consecration section up to [AND including] the memorial acclamation; memorial section up to [but NOT including] the final doxology; the final doxology and Amen). As a result, one sees the unity of this most important of all the prayers of the Mass constantly being compromised. For example, many presiding priests will announce, AFTER the *Sanctus,* which "eucharistic prayer" they are using, even though they are already part-way through the eucharistic prayer. Similarly, at concelebrations, after the memorial acclamation, sometimes a principal celebrant will have only one of the concelebrants (contrary to the rubrics) read the next section of the prayer (i.e., the anamnesis and communion-epiclesis). Or, frequently, there is a significant time gap between the end of the intercessions and the beginning of the doxology while the presiding priest is getting the paten and chalice in his hands and even inviting the assembly to "join me in reciting the 'Through him.…'" (This latter practice is now explicitly prohibited by GIRM #236.) Any of these practices destroys the sense that the eucharistic prayer is ONE prayer (albeit with several different parts).

If an announcement is necessary, it should occur BEFORE the preface dialogue. It should be noted that this is one of the places mentioned in the missal (GIRM #31) and the Directory for Masses with Children (#22, DOL–2155) as appropriate for the presiding priest to give a brief admonition (and to invite the assembly to think of motives for thanksgiving)![16]

Never break the host at the words of institution.

Breaking the host during the eucharistic prayer while saying "He broke the bread, gave it to his…" telescopes together two distinct actions in the Liturgy of the Eucharist—*blessing* and *breaking*—and tries to turn liturgical remembrance into dramatic reenactment. In addition, it is not even correct dramatic reenactment, since, by almost every theology around, the bread is not really "blessed" (i.e., consecrated) until AFTER the point at which certain priests break it. This practice, therefore, instead of imitating Scripture more closely, actually reverses the order found therein (i.e., BLESSING, then BREAKING is turned into BREAKING, then BLESSING).

Father Aidan Kavanagh is very strong in his dislike of those who break the host at an incorrect time. He writes the following:

The president of the assembly is not a mimic whose task is to reproduce the Last Supper. He is a servant who serves the assembly in its celebration of the Eucharist by proclaiming in its midst the motives for which it gives thanks. That on the night before he died, Jesus took bread, said the blessing, broke and gave it to his friends is a central motive for the assembly's giving thanks to God, but, as the Eucharistic Prayer itself makes clear, it is not the only one. The Eucharist is not a mnemonic tableau of an historical event. It is a sweeping thanksgiving for the whole of the Father's benevolence toward the world and his people in Christ and the Holy Spirit.

It does no more than what Jesus did in all the meals he took with those he loved. What he did at those meals quite escaped the bounds of any one meal on any one occasion. What he did was to make human beings free and forgiven table partners with God. Mimicking the details of what Jesus did at only one of those meals thus historicizes a mystery which transcends time and place, saying in the process far too little rather than too much. Christian liturgy is not an historical pageant. Presidents who cannot be convinced of this should not preside.[17]

The late Ralph Keifer agreed with Father Kavanagh's perceptions:

Breaking the host at the institution narrative is an abuse because the narrative is mainly a recital of why we celebrate the Eucharist (because this is the way the Lord Jesus has given us to regularly share together and celebrate his presence and power to transform us), not a demonstration of what we do at Eucharist. If the narrative were a demonstration of what we do, it would be appropriate not only to break the bread, but also to eat it at that point, and, the words having been said over the cup, to share that at this point also. The institution narrative is not designed to be a liturgical show-and-tell. It is designed, rather, to say that we celebrate the Eucharist because it is the memorial of the Lord.[18]

Let me also point out that some scholars conjecture that very early eucharistic prayers did not have the institution narrative within the eucharistic prayer (as is currently the case with the eucharistic prayer of Saints Addai and Mari used by the Assyrian Church of the East). Thus, it would have been impossible to break the bread during the institution narrative when using such prayers. The Canadian *Bulletin* several times reminds presiders to follow the rubrics and not to think that moving the breaking of bread leads to better liturgy.[19] For some reason, this seems to be a phenomenon that some priests continue to practice and for which there is no justification among any of the writings of liturgical experts.

Be careful about what is done with the doxology of the eucharistic prayer.

The doxology of the eucharistic prayer is still part of the presidential prayer, and thus should be proclaimed by the presiding priest alone (although at concelebrations, the concelebrants *may* join him, but are not obliged to do so [cf. GIRM #236]). That this section of the eucharistic prayer is the sole domain of priests was reiterated by the 1980 Instruction *Inæstimabile Donum* which states (#4): "The doxology itself is reserved to the priest." This is preceded a few sentences earlier by the statement, "It is therefore an abuse to have some parts of the Eucharistic Prayer said by the deacon, by a lower minister or by the faithful."[20] The prohibition against anyone other than concelebrating priests joining in the doxology is now explicitly included in the GIRM (#236).

In spite of such prohibitions, however, it is not an uncommon practice for some assemblies to join the priest (sometimes at his invitation) in reciting the doxology. Practically, this tends to trivialize the Great Amen to a whisper, yet it does help many in the assembly feel that they are adequately affirming the eucharistic prayer. In addition, at least among the Maronite Rite Catholics from Lebanon, the final phrase of the doxology of the eucharistic prayer ("now and always and forever") is communally recited, indicating that the practice is in the realm of liturgical possibility. In addition, the Maronites also communally recite a doxology during the breaking of the bread which immediately follows the eucharistic prayer and precedes the Lord's Prayer.

Nevertheless, all things being equal, in the Roman Rite, the presiding priest should not invite the assembly to join him in reciting the doxology (since it does break up the unity of this presidential prayer) and, instead, should foster efforts to enhance the Great Amen which follows.

If there is an assisting deacon, he should lift the chalice during the doxology, rather than the presiding priest. (In the absence of a deacon, a concelebrant *may* also lift the chalice [cf. GIRM #208]). The priest who presides, however, always holds the *bread* (cf. GIRM #180).

In addition, the current appropriate gesture with the consecrated elements is that the consecrated bread on the paten (or in an appropriate larger vessel) and a single chalice are held at about equal heights. The gesture that had been common in the Tridentine Mass, in which the host was held vertically *over* the chalice, was changed in 1969 and has *not been reintroduced* by any recent revision of the GIRM. It is permitted to hold a piece of the broken consecrated bread over the chalice when inviting the assembly to Communion (after the *Agnus Dei*), but holding the consecrated bread over the chalice during the doxology is NOT appropriate (as well as being *contrary to the rubrics*).

One final comment pertains to the height of the offerings during the doxology. Some scholars have found ancient texts which indicate that this is the high point of the eucharistic prayer—theoretically and physically (that is, visually). This is the major "physical" elevation. This is the point for the visible "offering." This is the point at which the gesture of offering gifts to heaven found in the Hebrew Scriptures should be imitated. Unfortunately, many priests are still under the impression that the height formerly prescribed in the Tridentine Missal (a few inches) should be continued now. The contrary is true.

The current missal says that the paten and chalice should be "elevated" during the doxology (GIRM ##151, 180), and evidence suggests that the doxology is the time for the grand gesture of lifting high the gifts toward heaven for all to see.

Do not trivialize the "great" Amen.

St. Jerome and other early authors mention the importance of the concluding Amen to the eucharistic prayer, and how it sounded like thunder in the city of Rome, shaking all the pagan temples.[21] In most churches nowadays, however, this Amen is more of a whimper than anything approximating thunder. Oftentimes this is due to the presiding priest's not saying the doxology of the eucharistic prayer in such a way that it elicits a response by the people. Whatever the cause, the problem needs to be cured.

The presiding priest should not "distribute" the sign of peace to the assembly.

At one point in the development of the Mass of the Roman Rite, the "Peace" was received from the altar by the presiding priest (when he kissed the altar at this point), and then passed to the deacon, who in turn passed it to the subdeacon, etc. The present missal has tried to abolish this hierarchical "trickle-down" clerical practice in favor of everyone in the assembly exchanging the peace immediately with those closest. There is no sense that the presiding priest is "the sole" minister of peace in the assembly. Yet this is what is symbolized when a presider walks throughout a church, trying to greet someone in every pew. The presiding priest has already greeted everyone via the liturgical greeting, "The peace of the Lord be with you always."

He need not greet anyone aside from those around him and, in fact, the GIRM now exhorts the presiding priest to remain in the sanctuary "so as not to disturb the celebration" (#154). Exceptions may be made in special circumstances (e.g., weddings, funerals). But, for a presiding priest to greet a large number of people on a regular basis tends to prolong this section of the liturgy unreasonably and obscure the fact that TAKING and BLESSING should *soon* be followed by BREAKING and GIVING.

Do not ignore the breaking of the bread.

The *Agnus Dei* accompanies the *significant action* of the breaking of the bread. The breaking of the bread does not accompany the *insignificant recitation* of the minor litany: "Lamb of God,…." In other words, what is important is that the breaking of the bread be seen by the assembly as a section of the liturgy as important as the preparation of the gifts, the eucharistic prayer and the Communion rite. In Luke's Gospel, and in the Acts of the Apostles, we have direct references to the "breaking of the bread" with eucharistic implications. This action is of immense significance! Yet, one often sees presiding priests who sneak the breaking of bread in while the kiss of peace is still continuing. Such a practice leads to a poorer experience and understanding of sharing in the one bread and one cup for all present. In addition, it should be noted that striking the breast during the *Agnus Dei* is no longer prescribed, and thus should be omitted.[22]

The presiding priest ought to minister Communion personally.

One of the key functions of the presiding priest is to proclaim the eucharistic prayer and, by implication, this task includes the action intimately related to the reason for the eucharistic prayer—ministering the Sacred Elements.[23] The 1980 Instruction *Inæstimabile Donum* also calls into question the practice that had occurred here and there, namely, of the presiding priest sitting during the Communion of the faithful while lay ministers take over "the unimportant task, which the priest doesn't really have to do." In fact, the 1980 Instruction is very strong in saying (#10) "a reprehensible attitude is shown by those priests who, though present at the celebration, refrain from distributing Communion and leave this task to the laity." The 2002 GIRM explicitly notes that it is when other priests are not present at Mass that extraordinary ministers may assist in ministering Communion (#162) and this general principle is included in the revised U.S. Norms for Communion under Both Kinds (#28), approved in March 2002. Serving as a minister of Communion is neither unimportant, nor is it a function of priests and deacons that may be delegated to laity without sufficient reasons. It is a task intimately connected with their function during the Liturgy of the Eucharist. It is a continuation of their role in the church as primary ministers of God's mysteries.

Do not change the rite of ministering Communion to make it more efficient and less personal.

In some places in the late 1970s, seemingly in the interests of efficiency, "self-intinction" had been practiced for Communion under both kinds and occasionally this practice continues. No major liturgical writer has ever suggested that intinction is a good way to minister Communion under both kinds—drinking from the chalice is always to be preferred (cf. U.S. Norms #42). One form of "self-intinction" forces all communicants to take a host themselves and then to dip it in the chalice. Such a practice does not give people the option of drinking from the chalice or even of receiving Communion on the tongue, and we must respect that piety even if we disagree with it. In addition, such a practice eliminates the necessity of having a minister in the action of receiving Communion, therefore depersonalizing it as well as turning an action which for centuries has been seen as "humbly receiving God's gifts" into "taking what is rightfully mine."

Archimandrite Robert Taft, S.J., an expert on liturgies of the Eastern Christian Churches, writes:

> But from the sources we have studied at least one thing is clear: the Eucharist, ideally at least, is not something one *takes*. It is a gift received, a meal shared. And since sacraments by their very nature are supposed to symbolize what they mean, then self-service, cafeteria-style communion rites just will not do.[24]

This same reorientation of symbol takes place anytime the Sacred Elements are passed through the congregation, as occasionally happens in some small group liturgies. Such a practice is also explicitly prohibited in the 2002 GIRM (#160).

The late Father Robert Hovda wrote:

> The personal sharing and transaction between minister and communicant is part of the symbolic action. That is why it is such a loss when that personal dimension is eliminated by the use of a mode of sharing which does not involve a minister of the plate and a minister of the cup. One sees this not infrequently: plates simply passed through a group, or cups simply placed on the altar to be found by communicants. The loss is not a minor one. It is a loss of personal eye contact, personal word, personal gesture, personal touch.[25]

If the group is small enough, it may be very meaningful, once in a while, for the presiding priest to minister the consecrated

Bread to all present first and then to minister the Precious Blood. But to pass the elements in a larger group, forcing everyone in a non-homogenous group to "take" rather than "receive," in the minds of most liturgical authors, results in a poorer liturgical experience.

Be sensitive to unimportant clerical-lay or male-female local "traditional" distinctions when arranging Communion ministers.

In some parishes only priests or deacons minister the bread, and the laity minister the chalice. Elsewhere, one sees men with the consecrated bread and women with the chalice. Should these distinctions be kept at Communion time? Traditionally, the presiding priest ministers the bread and the deacon the chalice, but when extraordinary lay ministers are used, there should be an equal mix (and an alternating mix) at the various Communion stations with men and women having an equal opportunity to minister either species.

Do not purify the vessels at the center of the altar. Do so at the side of the altar, or (even better) at the side table, or (ideally) wait until after Mass.

The revised U.S. Norms for Communion under Both Kinds (as well as the earlier U.S. document *This Holy and Living Sacrifice*) makes a distinction between consuming any of the consecrated elements that remain after Communion and *purifying* the vessels. Any of the Precious Blood that is left over is to be consumed *immediately* after Communion (U.S. Norms #52, cf. GIRM ##163, 182), and consecrated Bread is to be stored in a tabernacle or consumed (U.S. Norms #51, cf. GIRM #163).

The missal, however, does indicate a *preference* for purifying vessels after Mass ("especially if there are several vessels to be purified"—GIRM #163) at the credence table ("insofar as possible at the credence table"—GIRM #279).[26] If it seems absolutely necessary to cleanse the vessels immediately after Communion at the altar, it seems preferable that the priest stand *at the side,* rather than in the center.[27]

Do not have a litany of "thanksgiving" after Communion.

For a few years after the present Order of Mass was introduced in 1970, it was popular to fill in the meditative period after Communion with a "Litany of Thanksgiving." Reflection on this practice, however, has led liturgists to see it as less than ideal. The key moment for "thanksgiving" is the eucharistic prayer, and if there are particular items that need to be announced as reasons for special thanksgiving, they would most appropriately be mentioned immediately *before* the preface dialogue of the eucharistic prayer (NOT after Communion and also NOT during the prayer of the faithful). After Communion may be an appropriate time for a hymn of praise, but "a litany of thanksgiving" focuses energies away from the primary time of thanksgiving during the liturgy.

Do not make announcements before the prayer after Communion, thereby turning it into a preliminary blessing.

I grant that it is more convenient to make announcements when everyone is seated and quiet. Nevertheless, announcements do damage to the flow of the liturgy if done *before* the prayer after Communion and should properly come *after* this prayer. The post-Communion quiet is a period of reflection after encountering the Risen Christ through eating and drinking his body and blood in Communion. The prayer after Communion concludes this reflection and concludes the Communion procession, thereby also concluding the entire Liturgy of the Eucharist. The announcements, which regulations demand should be *brief* (GIRM ##90a, 166), are made to remind the assembly of significant major items, not lists of minutiae which can be read in the parish bulletin—and have nothing to do with Communion. They are looking out from the liturgy toward other activities—thus they should precede the final going-out which is the purpose of the Concluding Rites.

NOTES

1. Cf. *Certiores effecti,* sec. 3, #5 ff.

2. *Mediator Dei* #121.

3. *Constitution on the Liturgy* #55, DOL–55.

4. *Eucharisticum Mysterium* #31, DOL–1260.

5. 1969 GIRM #56h, DOL–1446h.

6. GIRM #85. The earlier text (1975 GIRM #56h) was changed by the addition of the words "just as the priest himself is bound to do" to make it explicit that the presiding priest must receive Communion from elements consecrated at that Mass. The 2002 GIRM thus states that the priest must receive from what is consecrated at that Mass and, in a similar way, "it is most desirable" that the people should be communicated from elements consecrated at that Mass "just as the priest himself is bound to do," thereby discouraging even more strongly the practice of resorting to what is in the tabernacle.

7. Cf. also Canadian *Bulletin,* v. 9, #54 (May–June, 1976), p. 174; v. 14, #77 (Jan.–Feb. 1981), p. 31.

8. Cf. O'Connell, *The Celebration of Mass,* p. 234.

9. Cf. Mueller, *Handbook of Ceremonies,* p. 84.

10. Although *The Rite of Dedication of a Church* does make mention of water being brought up in the procession with the offerings (e.g., Cpt II #72, Cpt III #32, Cpt IV #57, Cpt VII #12), the 2002 GIRM only mentions bread and wine (e.g., ##73, 140). (Appendix IV of the missal also mentions water, but it is taken from the *Dedication of a Church,* Cpt VII.)

11. Cf. BCL *Newsletter,* v. 8, ##7–8 (July–Aug. 1972), pp. 334–35. Also cf. rubrics in the Order of Mass.

12. Cf. Canadian *Bulletin,* v. 14, #77 (Jan.–Feb. 1981), p. 8.

13. Cf. BCL *Newsletter,* v. XX, ##4–5 (April–May. 1984), p. 16.

14. Cf. 2002 U.S. Norms for Communion Under Both Kinds #32.

15. The 2002 Latin edition of the Roman Missal typographically attempts to emphasize that the eucharistic prayer includes the preface by including the preface dialog and *Sanctus* with eucharistic prayers I and III (which do not have their own preface) and including a reference to the use of other prefaces.

16. Cf. *Eucharistiæ Participationem* # 8, DOL–1982.

17. Kavanagh, *Elements of Rite,* pp. 74–75.

18. Keifer, *To Give Thanks and Praise,* p. 140.

19. Cf. Canadian *Bulletin,* v. 9, #54 (May–June. 1976), p. 160, note 9; v. 14, #77 (Jan.–Feb. 1981), p. 16.

20. Cf. also note R37 to 1975 GIRM #191 in DOL–1581.

21. Jerome, *In Epist. ad Galat.* 2, *praef.,* PL 26:381.

22. Cf. DOL–1477, note R22.

23. Cf. Hovda, *Strong, Loving and Wise,* p. 36.

24. Taft, "Receiving Communion—A Forgotten Symbol?" p. 418.

25. Hovda, in Kay, *It Is Your Own Mystery,* pp. 31–32.

26. Cf. also GIRM #183.

27. Mention of purifying the vessels at the side of the altar was still included in 2000 GIRM #163, but "the side of" was omitted in the 2002 GIRM, possibly because many contemporary altars are relatively narrow

in width. Nevertheless, based on previous explanations from Rome, it seems that it is better to use the side of the altar for such a task, if the altar is wide enough. Cf. clarification regarding 1975 GIRM #238 in *Notitiæ*, v. 14 (1978), pp. 593–594; translation in DOL–1628: note R42.

THE CONCLUDING RITES

Do not change the role of the presiding priest by "blessing us" rather than "blessing you."

The importance of this minor change in pronouns may be a subject of great debate, but this topic should be raised because at least one noted liturgist sees significant implications when the formula for the final blessing is slightly altered so that the presiding priest says, "May almighty God bless *us,...*" instead of "May almighty God bless *you,....*" What can be so important and so significant about changing a pronoun from second person to first person? Isn't the presiding priest part of the assembly? Shouldn't God's blessings be sought for him also? Yes, the priest who presides is part of the assembled Christian community and, yes, God's blessings should be sought for him also. This, however, does not necessarily imply that in his role of presiding over the assembly he should include himself when asking God's blessings upon others. Excluding one's self when blessing others is a traditional format in our heritage—it is similar to the way that parents traditionally bless their children or the way that the patriarchs of the Hebrew Scriptures blessed others.

In a 1975 issue of *Living Worship,* the late Father Robert Hovda connected the rewording of the final blessing to the whole issue of presidential style (or lack of it). He wrote:

Without any desire to emulate them, we can sympathize with those priests who seem to shrink from the task of presiding at liturgical celebrations. We see them dropping out of sight whenever possible. We see them evidently embarrassed by their occupying a chair in our full view, or by the vesture that they wear with studied carelessness (as if to say "these things don't matter"). *We see them refusing the role by turning "you" to "us" in blessing, thus avoiding the personal confrontation so essential to good liturgical experience.* We see them forsaking any trace of reverential dignity for the sake of a nervous, giggly, phony chumminess. We see them presiding as if not presiding—in other words, rejecting their role of service.[1]

Granted Father Hovda seems to put the full weight of good presidential style on one pronoun in the blessing, but the implications that such a change makes in the liturgy as a whole are much broader than most people would suggest.

Do not bless "in the name of" the Father, etc.

As a priest, I absolve "in the name" of the Father, etc., and I baptize "in the name" of the Father, etc. Nevertheless, in the final blessing, the presiding priest is not, himself, blessing the people but, rather, asking God to bless them. Thus, as the presiding priest, I should not ask God that God would bless "in the name" of the Father, etc. God *cannot* bless "in the name" of anyone—God blesses "directly." The Latin version of the blessing *(Benedicat vos omnipotens Deus, Pater, et Filius, et Spiritus Sanctus)* is slightly clearer as to what is being expressed—unfortunately a literal translation leads to less than ideal English: "May [he] bless you, [the one who is] almighty God, [that is] Father, and Son, and Holy Spirit." When speaking words such as these, a priest is *not* bestowing a blessing (in his own name or in the name of anyone else). Rather, a priest is asking God that

God (Father, Son, and Spirit) bestow divine blessings on the assembly.

Do not omit "The Lord be with you" when using solemn blessings or prayers over the people.

Although the text of the greeting, "The Lord be with you," is not printed in the missal, the rubric printed there states that *the greeting* should be given by the presiding priest before the deacon says, "Bow your heads…" and the solemn blessing is pronounced.

NOTES

1. Hovda, "The Eucharistic Prayer Is More Than Words," *Living Worship,* v. 11, #4 (April 1975), p. 2 (emphasis added).

VARIA

TOPIC 1 – CONCELEBRATION

Concelebration is a liturgical rite and not a devotional practice.

Concelebration is a liturgical option. In this sense, it is similar to other options available, like the choice of the eucharistic prayer. Whether the option is chosen or not should depend on pastoral considerations.[1] The rubrics accompanying the three Eucharistic Prayers for Children flatly state that children's Masses should not be concelebrated (a directive I personally am not completely comfortable with).[2] In some liturgical families (i.e., the Byzantine Rite), all concelebrants must be at the altar for the eucharistic prayer (at least ideally); thus, it is sometimes necessary to limit the number of concelebrants. On the other hand, at least theoretically, the Ethiopian Rite *requires* about five concelebrants (preferably 7 and ideally 13) if the Eucharist is to be celebrated at all![3] The standard rubrics for a pontifical liturgy in the Byzantine Rite *require* a bishop to have at least one concelebrating priest. Symbolically, this binds the bishop to working with his priests, even in the celebration of the Eucharist!

At present in the Western church, concelebration is required only at episcopal and presbyteral ordinations, the blessing of an abbot, and the Chrism Mass (GIRM #199), and is discouraged only at children's liturgies. At other times, whether a concelebration is permitted and whether a given priest chooses to concelebrate is left to the judgment of the appropriate authority and the devotion of the individual priest. In the typical situation in the Western church, especially when there is no deacon, a concelebrant can often aid the total liturgical experience by proclaiming the Gospel, assisting at the altar, ministering Communion. Therefore, I personally would always encourage concelebrations rather than having priests celebrate "private" Masses or attend Mass *modo laico* (as a lay person). Concelebration is, in fact, also encouraged by the 2002 GIRM (#114).[4] This does not mean, however, that all priests present must concelebrate, and sometimes other concerns (such as avoiding liturgical "mob" scenes, avoiding a male-dominated liturgy, preserving a balance between "ministers" and "assembly") might suggest that it would be appropriate to limit the number of concelebrants.[5]

For many priests, however, particularly members of religious institutes who live in common, concelebration is a way of avoiding saying a private Mass or attending Mass, while also "getting daily Mass in." It is true that the official documents encourage concelebration,[6] but the reasoning given in the documents seems to be because of the sign value of the unity of the church—not because of the personal devotion of the priest. This distinction is important because, if taken seriously, it can influence the way various concelebrations may take place. It is the assembled church which should be the primary beneficiary of the liturgical rite—not primarily the devotion of the individual concelebrant.

Concelebration is not a committee presidency.

Any arrangement of concelebrants which reminds people of the board of directors versus the stockholders of a corporation should be avoided. Only one bishop or priest can preside.[7] Other bishops or priests present may concelebrate and, if they do, they liturgically function as needed to serve the entire assembly. They do not co-preside. Rather, they co-celebrate (as every baptized Christian present does) according to their episcopal or presbyteral rank. Co-celebrating (as ordained ministers) means that they can join in imposing hands over the elements and in QUIETLY reciting the central section of the eucharistic prayer. By so doing, they also join in consecrating the elements. This does not mean, however, that they are equal in liturgical function to the principal celebrant. The principal celebrant leads all present—including the concelebrants. In many respects, concelebrating priests are more a part of the assembly of the faithful than they are leaders of worship. Only the principal celebrant recites the presidential prayers, and only he should give the homily (although on special occasions, it may be appropriate for a concelebrant to give the homily).[8]

Concelebrants should be seen, but not necessarily heard.

The rubrics insist that the volume level of the concelebrants, especially during the eucharistic prayer, should be "very low" (*submissa voce*) (GIRM #218).[9] All the priests present do not act as if they were one huge Greek chorus. They should be seen, however. During the eucharistic prayer, they should be *near* the altar, but NOT *at* the altar (GIRM #215). The gesture of imposing hands during the invocation of the Spirit is the ONLY required gesture by a concelebrant and should normally be made with TWO hands (cf. GIRM #222a, *et passim*). The gesture at the words of the Lord are, in fact, *optional* (cf. GIRM #222c, *et passim*).[10]

The principal celebrant should be heard!

Many principal celebrants have developed the bad habit of lowering their voice during the common section of the eucharistic prayer. This practice makes it more awkward for other priests to concelebrate, since the concelebrants usually cannot hear the principal celebrant if he reduces his voice to a whisper. The requirement that all concelebrants recite the central sections of the eucharistic prayer exists in the present rite to satisfy the demands of current official theology (although some people have suggested that this communal recitation is actually bad liturgy). Yet, a concelebrated proclamation of the eucharistic prayer should never turn into a Greek-chorus type of proclamation. The principal celebrant must also preside during a concelebration and lead the concelebrating priests in prayer. To do this he must be heard! In general, the principal celebrant should actually raise his voice during the common section to make sure he is "clearly heard," not only by the concelebrants but also by the assembly during this most important of all prayers (cf. GIRM #218).[11]

The principal celebrant should not have two assistant chaplains, unless he is a bishop, in which case the two chaplains should be deacons.

At many concelebrations, one frequently sees three "major" concelebrants seated together. This practice is probably an unconscious imitation of the "three-priest Solemn High Mass" associated with the Tridentine Missal, with a bit of the "chaplains to the bishop" thrown in for good measure. Nowhere is it ever suggested that a simple priest need any assistants or chaplains at a concelebration. Concelebrants should all be seated together, APART from the principal celebrant. If assistance is needed because of a lack of other qualified ministers (deacons and acolytes), one or more of the concelebrants may help at the appropriate time, but they should not be seated together with the principal celebrant.

Only in the case where the principal celebrant is a bishop should there be "chaplains" seated on either side of him, and it is preferable that these chaplains be deacons, NOT concelebrating priests![12]

Do not delegate the anamnesis (memorial) section of the eucharistic prayer to only one concelebrant.

The missal (and introductions to the Eucharistic Prayers for Reconciliation and for Various Needs and Occasions) requires that *all* concelebrants together recite (quietly!) the eucharistic prayer from the consecratory epiclesis (invocation) through the consecration and anamnesis (memorial) to and *including the communion epiclesis* (GIRM #222, *et passim*). This section constitutes a bare-bones, "mini"-eucharistic prayer containing *all* parts common to all eucharistic prayers (and which are considered "essential" by many authors). Thus, according to present Roman Rite discipline, a concelebrant must recite all of his part (i.e., the entire "mini"-eucharistic prayer) to concelebrate licitly. Merely reciting the first half (up to the words of Christ), or merely reciting the words of consecration, is not enough to satisfy the rubrics (or ecumenical concerns).

I should also note that some renowned scholars (Karl Rahner, S.J., being one of them) have questioned the necessity of any co-vocalizing of sections of the eucharistic prayer.[13] Nevertheless, unless there is an official change in rubrics, all concelebrants should recite the memorial (anamnesis) and communion invocation (epiclesis) sections *after* the consecration as well as the invocation before.

On the other hand, it is not necessary to delegate any of the eucharistic prayer to concelebrants. A presiding priest may want to proclaim the entire prayer himself, and some authors suggest that this is actually a better liturgical practice.[14]

The basic symbol of the Eucharist is *one bread* and *one cup*. Therefore, only one paten and one chalice should be elevated at the doxology.

There is a common (though less than ideal) practice in which the two concelebrating "chaplains" to the principal celebrant elevate two chalices while the presiding priest himself elevates the bread. This seems to be done for the sake of symmetry (the same reasoning for having two "chaplains"). But this custom is based on a non-liturgical reason (i.e., "symmetry" or "balance"). The correct practice, however, is for the principal celebrant to raise the vessel of bread and the *deacon* to raise *the* chalice (since there should only be one chalice on the altar anyway) (cf. GIRM #180). (If there is no deacon present, *one* concelebrant *may* raise the chalice—GIRM #208.) This correct practice once again highlights the fundamental symbol of the Eucharist—*one bread* and *one cup*.

TOPIC 2 – FUNERALS

Do not begin twice.

In the English language *Order of Christian Funerals,* the Funeral Mass normally begins with the reception of the coffin at the door of the church.[15] The rite of reception is the formal beginning of the Mass. The usual act of penitence is omitted and the sign of the cross and greeting should both be done at the door of the church, preceding the sprinkling and clothing of the coffin. When the procession reaches the sanctuary, the presiding priest continues with (a simple welcome to those present on behalf of the family of the deceased and then) the collect.

Never turn the homily into a eulogy.

The Roman Missal specifically forbids a eulogy at a Catholic funeral (GIRM #382). Nevertheless, it continues to be a common occurrence to hear praises of the deceased as if the funeral were actually a canonization rite. The homily must be based on Scripture, but also should not neglect the life of the particular Christian who died. It should encourage the assembly to a deeper faith in eternal life, based on the faith of Christ who found life through his own death on the cross. The homilist should not ignore the connection between the death of a Christian and the death of Christ, and thus fail to use the funeral liturgy as a faith-building experience for the local Christian assembly.

The *Order of Christian Funerals* does allow a family member to say a few words of remembrance before the final commendation, at the end of the liturgy.[16] This may be an appropriate time for a few familial remembrances, but again, it should not turn into a list of reasons for canonizing the deceased.

Do not end twice.

The Funeral Mass ends with the "Amen" responding to the prayer after Communion. The Concluding Rites are *omitted* (i.e., the greeting, blessing, and dismissal) and, *in their place*, the Final Commendation and procession to the grave take place.

Do not turn the Final Commendation into a series of "absolution" prayers.

The Final Commendation, which takes place after the prayer after Communion, has a very simple structure: Invitation to Prayer, Song of Farewell, Prayer of Commendation. This rite is followed by the procession from the church to the grave. The former (1971 U.S.) version of the revised funeral rites *tolerated* merely recited invocations only if there were NO POSSIBLE WAY TO SING AN APPROPRIATE "FAREWELL" SONG. The current edition assumes that a Song of Farewell will always be sung and provides no alternative texts for communal recitation.

The main purpose of the Final Commendation is to bid farewell in song to the deceased—it is not an "absolution," trying to add more prayers to the greatest prayer possible—the eucharistic prayer! The Introduction to the revised funeral rites states that this Song of Farewell should be experienced as *the climax and high point* of the entire funeral rite.[17] The song is introduced by a brief opening invitation by the priest and concluded by a prayer of commendation, but these two texts should be seen as "brackets" for the primary liturgical action—singing the Song of Farewell.

Unfortunately, this section of the liturgy is usually experienced as a strange mixture of quasi-magical rites (water and incense), unknown responses (who remembers the exact wording of "Saints of God, come to his aid…"?), and more wordy prayers. This is NOT good liturgy (besides being illegal!). Appropriate "Farewell" hymns can be found in contemporary hymnbooks, set to tunes that can be used even with most heterogeneous funeral congregations.[18] If a hymn is actually sung as the rubrics require, the text of "Saints of God" is not to be recited in addition to the hymn!

During the singing of the Song of Farewell, the remains may be sprinkled with holy water and incensed, but neither is mandatory. In fact, the rubrics suggest that if holy water was used at the beginning of the liturgy, its use would ordinarily be omitted during the Final Commendation.

NOTES

1. Cf. 1983 *Code of Canon Law,* canon 902.

2. Introduction to the Eucharistic Prayers for Children #22, DOL–2020.

3. Taft, *Ex Oriente Lux?,* p. 310.

4. The text in the 2002 GIRM merely restates the exhortations contained in the 1967 document, *Eucharisticum Mysterium,* especially ##43 and 47, DOL–1272, 1276. Also see the 1999 U.S. Guidelines for the Concelebration of the Eucharist #6.

5. Cf. Archbishop Hunthausen, "Male and Female God Created…," Pastoral Recommendations #7, "We will continue our effort to avoid male dominance in liturgical settings,…by using care concerning the appropriateness of concelebrations,…"; cf. also the 1978 U.S. Bishops' Committee on the Liturgy Study Text 5, *Eucharistic Concelebration,* section V, pp. 19–23, "Concelebration is never presented…as a way of dealing with large numbers of priests…there are occasions when the number of concelebrants will need to be limited…."; GIRM #202 gives the bishop the authority to regulate concelebration in his diocese. See the 1999 U.S. Guidelines for Concelebration, ##8, 9.

6. Cf. *Eucharisticum Mysterium* #47, DOL–1276. GIRM #114. cf. 1999 U.S. Guidelines for Concelebration #6.

7. 1999 U.S. Guidelines for Concelebration #12.

8. Cf. also 1978 BCL Study Text 5, *Eucharistic Concelebration.*

9. Cf. also footnote R36 at DOL–1558.

10. Cf. also footnote R36 at DOL–1558.

11. Cf. also footnote R36 at DOL–1558.

12. Cf. *Ceremonial of Bishops* ##26, 128.

13. Cf. J. McGowan, *Concelebration,* pp. 77 ff.

14. Cf. Smolarski, *Eucharistia,* pp. 140–41.

15. The 1985 *Order of Christian Funerals* (approved by the Vatican for the United States in 1987 and published in 1989) is a revised

English translation, with minor adaptations, of the 1969 revised Latin Funeral rites.

16. In Canada, such a remembrance of the departed may take place during a Vigil Service, but not at the end of the Mass.

17. Introduction to the 1969 *Ordo Exsequiarum* #10, DOL–3382. Also see *Order of Christian Funerals* (U.S. edition), #147.

18. E.g., "Song of Farewell" in *Gather* (1994, GIA Publications [#864]), *I Am the Resurrection and the Life: Resources for Christian Funerals* (1994, Oregon Catholic Press), *Music for Christian Funerals* (1990, World Library Publications); also see Appendix I; also cf. 1985 *Order of Christian Funerals* (U.S. edition), #396 E, #403.5, and *The Liturgy of the Hours,* Office for the Dead, Evening Prayer, Alternative Hymn.

WHAT TO DO?

Now that this book has been read (or skimmed), what should those who preside do (or what should a liturgy committee do to help the presiders in their parish) to improve a liturgy? I wish there were a simple answer to this question; the author of the answer would be canonized for making a great contribution to the spiritual life of the church, besides becoming a millionaire in this life! But there is no simple answer. In some cases, helping others to improve their liturgies may be as difficult as trying to teach willing and hopeful teenagers how to be great actors—the willingness is there, but the techniques need much development.

Yet, before we try to *do* anything, perhaps there are preliminary steps that need to be taken. Too often, in our enthusiasm and eagerness, we humans rush to *do* first and only later do we take the time to stop and reflect. In Luke's Gospel, the narrative of the institution of the Eucharist contains the command of Jesus, "Do this in memory of me" (Luke 22:19). *Doing* is linked to *remembering.* Perhaps, in the ongoing task of liturgical renewal, as in many other areas of our lives, human activity might be more fruitful if we paused to remember and reflect before plodding, unreflectively, ever onwards toward our elusive goal. And we should remember not to try to escape to the past, for there is no return to those "good old days." The world continues to change and, even though our faith in Jesus is based on unchanging truths, the way we express and celebrate that faith is tempered by the times and culture in which we live. Jesus commands us, as he commanded Mary Magdalene, "Stop holding on to me…" (John 20:17), for we are always to celebrate and proclaim his risen life to the world in which we *now* live.

Often, when *remembering*, it can be helpful to review the past so as to put things into some historical perspective. Such reflection enables us to see what has occurred and what yet remains to be accomplished. The Liturgical Movement, the 1947 papal encyclical *Mediator Dei* on the liturgy, the revision of the rites of Holy Week by Pope Pius XII in the 1950s, and the Second Vatican Council (with the subsequent revision of the Mass, sacraments, and other liturgical rites), were some of the great events related to liturgy that took place during the twentieth century. We now live in the twenty-first century and many significant global events have taken place since the Second Vatican Council: the emergence of the Internet, the collapse of the Soviet Union, and the tragic destruction of New York's World Trade Center on September 11, 2001 being just three among many. In addition, each of us can probably name other significant events that have occurred in our personal history and which affect the way we view our world. All these events provide special incentives to pause and reflect on our progress (or lack thereof) in various areas of human life.

In particular, the publication of the third edition of the Roman Missal in Latin in March 2002 with its revised GIRM, and the 40th anniversary of the promulgation of the *Constitution on the Sacred Liturgy* in December 2003, provide Catholics special opportunities to reflect on their experience of eucharistic and other liturgical celebrations. In comparison with the numerous major changes that took place when Mass began to be celebrated in the vernacular in 1964 and the 1969 revised Order of Mass was introduced in the early 1970s, as mentioned in the Prenotes the specific rubrical changes contained in this latest edition of the missal are relatively few and minor. Several of the changes in the 2002 GIRM, however, call us to reflect on some fundamental practices. For example, there is a continued focus on the presidential chair even at a Mass with only one minister present (GIRM #256); there is added encouragement for ministering Communion from what is consecrated at that Mass (GIRM #85); by allowing the priest to hold the host over the chalice at the invitation to Communion and permitting the diocesan bishop to establish norms regarding Communion under both kinds, there is an assumption that Communion will be regularly distributed from the chalice (GIRM ##157, 283); by explicitly noting that some texts may be "sung" as well as "said" (e.g., GIRM ##125, 126, 137) and by explicitly encouraging singing on Sundays and holidays (GIRM #40), additional emphasis is given to singing during the liturgy. These few examples all point to fundamentals of liturgy that everyone would do well to reflect upon on a regular basis.

But sometimes remembering principles and history alone is only one step to help renewal. A recalling of *theory* must be accompanied by a review of *practice*. Hence, an equally important step consists in an honest self-examination (à la an examination of conscience) about what actually is being done during the celebration of Mass in our parishes or communities, and such a self-examination quite often needs a "second set of eyes."

In his poem "To a Louse," Robert Burns gives us these oft-quoted words:

O wad some Pow'r the giftie gie us,
to see oursels as others see us!

Along with the thoughts of Burns, let us also consider the following maxim based on a saying of Our Lord, as recorded in the Gospel of Matthew (13:9):

Whoever has *eyes*
ought to *see.*

Much improvement can occur in our lives and our liturgies if we can somehow remove our blind spots and see our imperfections the way others do, with a "second set of eyes." Thus, as important as it is to reflect on liturgical principles (and reread the GIRM), it is equally important to take practical steps "to see oursels as others see us." Perhaps the following suggestions might be helpful to that end.

First of all, priests who have been ordained for a number of years might risk having themselves videotaped during a typical Mass, or even a special "dry" Mass. Videotaping is a technique in common use in seminaries today as part of a liturgy training class for prospective priests, and certainly it would be a rare parish in which several families did not own their own portable video camcorders and VCRs. In seminary courses, after a taping of a "Mass," one or more professors and one or more peers critique the "presiding priest" and make suggestions, not only to point out rubrics whose spirit or letter were not quite fulfilled, but also to help the future priest become more natural, more human in gestures, in the same way that an actor is helped by a drama coach to become more natural in a dramatic role. The same critique can also be accomplished without a television camera by using a trusted friend with that "second set of eyes," but videotaping has the advantage of letting the presider "see ourselves as others see us" if he is someone who "has eyes" as the poem and maxim go.

In order to improve gestures (and other aspects of style), one suggestion given by a seminary professor in a "how to" liturgy class was that future priests "say Mass" in front of a full-length (or full-wall) mirror *without* any words, and try to let their *gestures* and *body language* do the "talking." A critique based on this technique can be very enlightening. Did a given gesture convey the meaning of the unspoken text? Why or why not? How can this be improved? (One can also do this via video-tape by turning off the sound!)

Another suggestion for veteran priests is to visit other churches and attend Mass, primarily to learn from another priest what may or may not be helpful in leading others in prayer. It is a rare occurrence for some priests to be at a Mass presided over by another. This experience may be an eye-opener to some. (Why is he doing that? Could I be wrong?) To others, it may be excruciatingly painful. (Will this awful homily *never* end? I wonder if I preach *that* poorly?)

Finally, it may be good for each priest (as well as each deacon or parish liturgy coordinator), once a year, to reread the *General Instruction of the Roman Missal* and the detailed rubrics in the Order of Mass in order to recall what should or should not be done. Any such reading should not only focus on reviewing the actual rubrics, but also on understanding the principles and spirit behind the rubrics. Rereading the GIRM can be enlightening. For, once we get ourselves into a pattern, it is hard to detect and then break the pattern, even if it is incorrect. Nevertheless, the worship of the Lord and the service of God's people deserve our best efforts.

The rubrics in the Roman Missal are like a recipe for a fine pastry. Following or ignoring the rubrics (or the recipe) will not automatically guarantee success or failure. But overlooking basic principles can lead to disaster—one does not substitute salt for sugar just because they look the same.

This book is an attempt to help those who preside and all who work with the liturgy become more sensitive to authentic liturgical traditions as found in the Roman Rite, especially as revised after the Second Vatican Council. Following the suggestions presented here will not automatically guarantee a "perfect" Mass nor will it eliminate all problems. But becoming sensitive to the principles behind the suggestions presented here may help all of us realize that worship of our God is more than minimally correct actions and an avalanche of words. It is a human interaction, an affair of the heart, a combined effort of all believers who are assembled together, each leading the others to a deeper love of the Divine Lover and to a deeper commitment toward one another, as they share the Bread of Life and the Cup of Eternal Salvation.

APPENDIX I

The following are two versions of the Song of Farewell, as given in the *Order of Christian Funerals.* Both are translations of the old Latin hymn *Subvenite,* and are set to two different, but standard, English language musical meters, and thus they can be sung according to various commonly recognized melodies. [Italicized pronouns should be changed in gender and number as the situation requires.]

METRICAL VERSION A—LONG METER (88.88)

Come to *his* aid, O saints of God;
Come, meet *him,* angels of the Lord.
Receive *his* soul, O holy ones;
present *him* now to God, Most High.

May Christ, who called you, take you home,
and angels lead you to Abraham.
Receive *his* soul, O holy ones;
present *him* now to God, Most High.

Give *him* eternal rest, O Lord.
May light unending shine on *him.*
Receive *his* soul, O holy ones;
present *him* now to God, Most High.

(Optional additional verse)
   I know that my Redeemer lives,
   the last day I shall rise again.

Receive *his* soul, O holy ones;
present *him* now to God, Most High.

Familiar melodies
> Old Hundredth ("Praise God, from Whom All Blessing Flow")
> *O Salutaris Hostia*

or by doubling the last two lines of each verse,
88.88.88 melodies
St. Catherine ("Faith of Our Fathers")
Melita ("Almighty Father, Strong to Save"—Navy Hymn)

METRICAL VERSION B—COMMON METER (86.86)

Come to *his* aid, O saints of God;
O angels, meet *him* now.
Receive *his* soul, present *him* now
to God, the Lord Most High.

May Christ, who called you, take you home;
Near Abr'am may you rest.
Receive *his* soul, present *him* now
to God, the Lord Most High.

Give *him* eternal rest, O Lord;
May *he* have endless light.
Receive *his* soul, present *him* now
to God, the Lord Most High.

(Optional additional verse)
> I know that my Redeemer lives;
> The last day I shall rise.

Receive *his* soul, present *him* now
to God, the Lord Most High.

Familiar melodies
Amazing Grace
St. Anne ("O God, Our Help in Ages Past")
St. Flavian ("These Forty Days of Lent")

APPENDIX II

GIRM Cross References

As noted earlier, all references to the GIRM in this edition are to the 2002 GIRM as contained in the 3rd edition of the Roman Missal. For those who do not have access to the 2002 GIRM in the vernacular or who wish to reference the earlier editions of the GIRM, the following table provides cross-references to those paragraphs noted in the text. Note that the correspondence between the 2002 GIRM and the 1975 GIRM is often approximate since, in several cases, significant changes have been introduced in the 2002 version.

2002 GIRM	1975 GIRM	DOL Reference Number (for 1975 GIRM)
24	[new to 2002 GIRM]	
31	11	1401
32	12	1402
40	19	1409
45	23	1413
48	26	1416
56	[new to 2002 GIRM] [cf. Intro. Lect. 28]	
58	[new to 2002 GIRM]	

2002 GIRM	1975 GIRM	DOL Reference Number (for 1975 GIRM)
59	34	1424
63c	39	1429
65	41	1431
72	48	1438
73	49	1439
75	49, 51	1439, 1441
78	54	1444
85	56h	1446h
90	57	1447
91	58	1448
99	66	1456
105	68	1458
111	73	1463
114	76	1466
122	84	1474
124	86	1476
125	87	1477
126	87	1477
132	93	1483
133	94	1484
134	95	1485
136	97	1487

2002 GIRM	1975 GIRM	DOL Reference Number (for 1975 GIRM)
137	98	1488
138	cf. 99	cf. 1489
140	101	1491
141	102	1492
142	103	1493
145	106	1496
151	[new to 2002 GIRM]	
154	112	1502
157	115	1505
160	117	1507
162	[new to 2002 GIRM]	
163	120	1510
166	123	1513
175	131	1521
178	133	1523
180	135	1525
182	137	1527
183	138	1528
199	153	1543
202	155	1545
206	156	1546
208	160	1550

2002 GIRM	1975 GIRM	DOL Reference Number (for 1975 GIRM)
212	164	1554
215	167	1557
218	170	1560
222	174	1564
236	191	1581
256	[new to 2002 GIRM]	
274	233 [CB 69]	1623
279	238	1628
281	240	1630
282	241	1631
283	242	1632
298	[new to 2002 GIRM] [cf. CIC 1235.2, Ded. Church IV. 6]	
306	[new to 2002 GIRM]	
308	270	1660
309	272	1662
315	[new to 2002 GIRM]	
318	278	1668
321	283	1673
352	313	1703
365	322	1712
382	338	1728

BIBLIOGRAPHY

Baldovin, S.J., John F. "Concelebration: A Problem of Symbolic Roles in the Church," *Worship*, v. 59, n. 1 (Jan. 1985), pp. 32–47.

Bouley, O.S.B., Allen. *From Freedom to Formula: The Evolution of the Eucharistic Prayer from Oral Improvisation to Written Texts* (Studies in Christian Antiquity, v. 21). Washington, DC: Catholic University Press, 1981.

Bugnini, Annibale. *The Reform of the Liturgy 1948–1975.* Collegeville, Minn.: The Liturgical Press, 1990.

Built of Living Stones. Washington: United States Catholic Conference, 2000.

Cabié, Robert. *The Church at Prayer (Vol. II): The Eucharist.* Collegeville, Minn.: The Liturgical Press, 1986.

Certiores effecti, Encyclical letter to the Italian Bishops, Pope Benedict XIV, November 13, 1742.

Champlin, Joseph M. *The Proper Balance.* Notre Dame, Ind.: Ave Maria Press, 1981.

Directory for Masses with Children, Sacred Congregation for Divine Worship, November 1, 1973.

Documents on the Liturgy: 1963–1979—Conciliar, Papal, and Curial Texts. Collegeville, Minn.: The Liturgical Press, 1982.

Emminghaus, Johannes H. *The Eucharist: Essence, Form, Celebration.* Collegeville, Minn.: The Liturgical Press, 1978.

Environment and Art in Catholic Worship, Bishops' Committee on the Liturgy, National Conference of Catholic Bishops, 1978.

Eucharistiæ Participationem, Letter to the Presidents of the National Conferences of Bishops concerning Eucharistic Prayers. Sacred Congregation for Divine Worship, April 27, 1973.

Eucharistic Concelebration. Bishops' Committee on the Liturgy, Study Text 5.

Eucharisticum Mysterium, Instruction. Sacred Congregation of Divine Worship, May 27, 1967.

Fulfilled In Your Hearing: The Homily in the Sunday Assembly. Bishops' Committee on Priestly Life and Ministry, National Conference of Catholic Bishops, 1982.

Guidelines for Concelebration of the Eucharist. Bishops' Committee on the Liturgy, 1999. (Available online at: http://www.usccb.org/liturgy/current/concel.htm)

Guzie, Tad W. *The Book of Sacramental Basics.* New York: Paulist Press, 1982.

Hovda, Robert W. *Strong, Loving and Wise: Presiding in Liturgy.* Collegeville, Minn.: The Liturgical Press, 1976, 1980.

Huck, Gabe. *Sunday Mass Five Years from Now.* Chicago: Liturgy Training Publications, 2001.

Huels, John M. *Disputed Questions in the Liturgy Today.* Chicago: Liturgy Training Publications, 1988.

Huels, John M. *More Disputed Questions in the Liturgy.* Chicago: Liturgy Training Publications, 1996.

Hunthausen, Most Rev. Raymond G., Archbishop of Seattle. "Male and Female God Created…: A Pastoral Statement on Women in the Church," October 2, 1980 (excerpts in *Catholic Mind,* September, 1981).

Inæstimabile Donum, Instruction. Sacred Congregation for the Sacraments and Divine Worship, April 3, 1980.

Institutio Generalis Missalis Romani (2002). Latin text available at: http://www.usccb.org/liturgy/current/missalisromanilat.htm

Johnson, Lawrence J. *The Word & Eucharist Handbook.* San Jose: Resource Publications, Inc., 1986.

Jungmann, s.j., Joseph A. *The Mass of the Roman Rite: Its Origins and Development.* New York: Benziger Bros., 1959.

Kavanagh, O.S.B., Aidan. *Elements of Rite: A Handbook of Liturgical Style.* New York: Pueblo Publishing Co., 1982.

Kay, Melissa (ed.). *It Is Your Own Mystery: A Guide to the Communion Rite.* Washington, DC: The Liturgical Press, 1977.

Keifer, Ralph A. *To Give Thanks and Praise.* Washington, DC: National Association of Pastoral Musicians, 1980.

Living Worship. The Liturgical Conference. v. 11, #4 (April 1975).

Mahoney, Cardinal Roger. *Gathered Faithfully Together: Guide for Sunday Mass.* Chicago: Liturgy Training Publications, 1997.

Mediator Dei, Encyclical letter of Pope Pius XII. November 20, 1947.

McGowan, R.S.C.J., Jean Carroll. *Concelebration: Sign of Unity of the Church.* New York: Herder and Herder, 1964.

Mueller, S.J., John Baptist. *Handbook of Ceremonies: For Priests and Seminarians.* St. Louis, Mo.: B. Herder Book Co., 1958.

Music in Catholic Worship, Bishops' Committee on the Liturgy, National Conference of Catholic Bishops, Second Edition, 1983.

The Mystery of Faith: A Study of the Structural Elements of the Order of Mass, Washington, DC: The Federation of Diocesan Liturgical Commissions, 1980.

National Bulletin on Liturgy, Canadian Conference of Catholic Bishops.

Norms for the Celebration and Reception of Communion under Both Kinds in the Dioceses of the United States of America. United States Conference of Catholic Bishops, June 14, 2001. (Available at http://www.usccb.org/liturgy/current/norms.htm)

O'Connell, J. B. *The Celebration of Mass.* Milwaukee: The Bruce Publishing Co., 1964.

Pontificalia insignia, Motu Proprio. Pope Paul VI, June 21, 1968.

Power, David N. *Unsearchable Riches: The Symbolic Nature of the Liturgy.* New York: Pueblo Publishing Company, 1984.

A Reader: The Environment for Worship. Bishops' Committee on the Liturgy, National Conference of Catholic Bishops, 1980.

Regan, O.S.B., Patrick. "Liturgy and the Experience of Celebration," *Worship,* v. 47, n. 10 (Dec. 1973), pp. 592–600.

Smolarski, S.J., Dennis C. *Eucharistia: A Study of the Eucharistic Prayer.* New York: Paulist Press, 1982.

Smolarski, S.J., Dennis C. *The General Instruction of the Roman Missal 1969–2002: A Commentary.* Collegeville, Minn.: The Liturgical Press, 2003.

Smolarski, S.J., Dennis C. *Q&A: The Mass.* Chicago: Liturgy Training Publications, 2002.

Smolarski, S.J., Dennis C. *Sacred Mysteries: Sacramental Principles and Liturgical Practice.* New York: Paulist Press, 1995.

Taft, S.J., Robert. *"Ex Oriente Lux?* Some Reflections on Eucharistic Concelebration," *Worship,* v. 54, n. 4 (July 1980), pp. 308–325.

Taft, S.J., Robert. "Receiving Communion: the Forgotten Sign," *Worship,* v. 57, (1983), pp. 412–418.

This Holy and Living Sacrifice: Directory for the Celebration and Reception of Communion under Both Kinds, U.S. National Conference of Catholic Bishops, Nov. 1, 1984.

Turner, Paul. *A Guide to the General Instruction of the Roman Missal.* Chicago: Liturgy Training Publications, 2003.

Wagner, Nick. *Modern Liturgy Answers the 101 Most-Asked Questions about Liturgy.* San Jose: Resource Publications, Inc., 1996.

Walsh, S.S., Eugene A. *Practical Suggestions for Celebrating Sunday Mass.* Glendale, Ariz.: Pastoral Arts Associates of North America, 1978.